DANCERS IN THE SUNSET SKY

BOOKS BY ROBERT F. JONES

Blood Sport, 1974

The Diamond Bogo, 1977

Slade's Glacier, 1981

Blood Root, 1982

Blood Tide, 1990

The Fishing Doctor, 1991

Jake, 1992

Upland Passage, 1992

African Twilight, 1995

Tie My Bones to Her Back, 1996

DANCERS IN THE SUNSET SKY

THE MUSINGS OF A BIRD HUNTER

ROBERT F. JONES

LYONS & BURFORD, PUBLISHERS

Printed in the United States of America

Illustrations © by Leslie Watkins
Design by LaBreacht Design

10 9 8 7 6 5 4 3 2 1

Library of Congress Cataloging-in-Publication Data

Jones, Robert F., 1934–
    Dancers in the sunset sky : the musings of a bird hunter / Robert F. Jones.
        p.   cm.
    ISBN 1-55821-496-8
    1. Bird hunting. 2. Game and game-birds. 3. Jones, Robert F., 1934–
I. Title.
    SK313.J65   1996
    799.2′4—dc20   96-14177
                                                        CIP

"There is a solitude, or perhaps a solemnity, in the few hours that precede the dawn of day which is unlike that of any others in the twenty-four, and which I cannot explain or account for. Thoughts come to me at this time that I never have at any other. Often I have experienced the mental state to which I refer, and the locality or situation has nothing to do with it. It comes when looking for the morning flight of ducks or geese in the populous East, just as it does while waiting for light to see deer in Nebraska, or when on some lofty peak in the Rocky Mountains I await the dawn to discover the whistling elk, or the bighorn cropping the tender grass on the steep hillside. Others, too, are influenced, I think, by some similar sensation, for when I have a companion with me at such a time he is usually subdued and quiet, and when he speaks, does so below his breath, as though afraid of breaking the universal stillness."

George Bird Grinnell, 1879

CONTENTS

INTRODUCTION 9

Are You Lonesome Tonight? 17
A Story

RUSTY & BELLE 23

TWO TRAMPS IN MUD-TIME 35

GLORIOUS CARNAGE 41

CONNOISSEURS OF COVER 55

PARTNERS 61

THE BOGSUCKER NIGHTMARE 67

D-DAY IN MARYLAND 73

A DOG'S BEST FRIEND 85

THE TODD SEEBOHM SAGA 93

FURTHER ADVENTURES OF TODD 99

AMERICA'S BIRD 105

AN ENDLESS DEBATE 121

FOOL'S PARADISE 129

LESSONS FROM A BIRD FEEDER 137

MY GIRL FRIDAY 143

REVENGE 151

OPERATION FLEABAG 159

IT WOULDN'T BE THE SAME 165

WAMPUM ON WALL STREET 171

In the Drowned Lands 181
A Story

TO LOUISE

For forty years of love and valor

INTRODUCTION

"The woodcock is a living refutation
of the theory that the utility of a
game bird is to serve as a target, or to
pose gracefully on a slice of toast. No
one would rather hunt woodcock in
October than I, but since learning of
the sky dance I find myself calling
one or two birds enough. I must be
sure that, come April, there will be
no dearth of dancers in the sunset
sky. . . ."

So wrote Aldo Leopold, the great sage of contemporary conservation, back in 1948. He was referring to the annual spring spectacle of woodcock on their singing grounds. Each March, where I live in southern Vermont, the migrant woodcock return to the meadow behind my house, as they do to similar fields across their northern range from Maine to Minnesota, and begin staking out their territories, competing for mates, and breeding their succeeding generations. For the next two months, at dawn and dusk, their sky dance will brighten my life.

Their arrival spells the end of the grimmest time of year in these parts. It's mud season, winter's last laugh: the weather is wet and cold; the dirt road that leads to my house from the village five miles down the mountain lies axle-deep in gumbo, waiting to suck down small cars or even four-wheel-drive trucks. The anchor ice is out and the brook running past my back window, usually clear and chuckling through most of the year, now roars brown and scum-tongued and angry with runoff. The woods are black and skeletal with only a few die-hard oak leaves still hanging on, and the fields behind my house squat soggy and gray, the grass flattened by the weight of wind and winter. My once-robust woodpile has dwindled appallingly and the tarps that cover it hang loose and faded by the rigors of winter like the clothes of a wasted old man. A premature robin hops across the backyard, his feathers puffed against the chill, no doubt wondering why he's been so foolish as to push his way north before the frost is completely out of the ground. The sky hangs low on the encircling mountaintops, now and then spitting the last white invective of winter, and dirty skifts of snow still hang in the low places and on the north-facing slopes of Bear Mountain.

Then one evening at dusk I step out my back door and hear that familiar froglike croak—*brzzzt! brzzzt!*—from the far end of the meadow. It's followed by a cheery twittering as the bird launches itself into the air, spiraling upward out of the gloom until it catches the last pearly light of the setting sun. Then it tumbles back to earth, burbling a liquid song. Suddenly the oppression of winter lifts, a ray of sunshine stabs my cob-webbed heart, I grin hugely, and I dash back into the house to tell my wife, "The woodcock are back!"

To my way of thinking, all the birds we hunt are dancers in the sun-set sky. You can hunt the best of them—partridge and woodcock—at any hour of the day, but they're something magical in the twilight. Dusk is also the best time, both tactically and aesthetically, to kill certain other wildfowl—ducks and geese in whatever language or latitude, sand grouse or whitewing doves whistling in to water themselves in any dry, hot, thorny country, Africa or the Latinate lands below the border. Home coverts too are always at their best in low light. A cock pheasant, long-spurred and fiery-tailed, rattling up the sun with his metallic flight, the quickening whirr of his wings, then the thump of the gun and the thud of his fall—after that, who needs to smell the coffee?

I've hunted birds for more than half a century now, starting with prairie chickens and ruffed grouse, pheasants and snipe and woodcock, bluebills and sprig and snows and Canadas in Wisconsin where I grew up. Since then I've been lucky enough to see more than thirty species of them fly and fold in some twenty-six states, provinces, territories, districts, or shires of seven countries from Canada to Costa Rica, New Zealand to Kenya. Memories of those hunts and the lessons learned from them pervade this book, along with more recent experiences in new places with waterfowl and upland birds both domestic and foreign, wherever and whenever they fly.

Tastes change with time, enthusiasms wax and wane, yet my love for game birds and the pursuit of them is as strong now as it was the first time I chased them. Certainly, thanks to experience, it's a deeper love. I know a lot more about the habits and habitats of the birds I hunt than I did as a boy, starting out in the long-grass prairies and cutover forests of the Upper Middle West. I've learned the sometimes-subtle differences, almost amounting to personalities, among species. In the blur of action, especially in low light, a hen pheasant and a sharptail grouse look much the same when they flush, yet the speed and shallower wing-beats of the sharptail distinguish it instantly for me from its look-alike —a significant distinction in a place where both birds are fair game but only cock pheasants may be taken. Similarly, in dense cover a "legal" ruffed grouse and a protected spruce grouse get off the ground with the same heart-stopping roar of wings, but the longer tail of even a female ruff is the giveaway. Mallards and black ducks are genetic cousins, the blacks only a little darker and sometimes slightly larger, more heavily built, than mallard hens, yet the mallards will toll gladly and in numbers into your blocks, only too happy to join the party, while the shy, suspicious blacks circle the set warily, only a few at a time, more often than not declining the invitation. More power to them.

You'd think that anyone would be able to tell an owl from a woodcock, yet once, years ago, when I was hunting a dense, deeply shaded covert in central Michigan for grouse and woodcock, the fellow I was hunting with suddenly yelled, "Mark right!" I saw a dark, long-winged, woodcock-sized bird flash past me, dodging through the upper stories of the alder thicket with the high dihedral and agility of a woodcock. I upped and shot. But even as I hit the trigger, some dim part of my brain was wondering why I hadn't heard the distinctive woodcock whistle, caused by the bird's primary feathers in the rapid wingbeats of a flush. When I picked it up I had the answer. It was a screech owl—small, soft-feathered, its huge yellow eyes dimming in death—disturbed from its midday slumber in the alder brake, and to this day I sorely regret having murdered it, out of bloodlust and a desire to show off in front of another man, as much as I would had I accidentally shot my hunting partner. Such mistakes are the mortal sins of my religion.

And it *is* a religion, older, deeper, and more visceral than Judaism or Christianity or even Islam, as old at least as the Pleistocene cave paintings of the Dordogne or Altamira. It has its own prayers, of thanks coupled with a plea for forgiveness each time we kill what we seek; its own dark sacraments and rituals and symbols; its own distinctive art.

The high priests of this religion are our gundogs, and learning how to follow their bidding in the field is no small art in itself. Though they won't be able to appreciate my saying so in print, I owe an enormous debt of gratitude to the gundogs that have shared my life over the years: the Irish setters, Rusty and Belle, who set me on this trail nearly half a century ago; Max, the German shorthair, who was superb at his trade; my various lovable Labradors, Peter, Simba, Buck, Luke, and Jake. Luke was the best of them, perhaps the keenest hunter I've ever known, but Jake already ranks right up there beside him, having learned much of what he knows from Luke. Then, of course, there's my Jack Russell terrier, Roz, whom Jake has somehow taught to be a bird dog, though she sometimes practices the art in a wild and crazy way all her own. You'll read about her later in this book, along with all of the others.

In the beginning, for me at least and humbly enough, there was a bird-shooting scene done in 1874 by Thomas Eakins. I first saw it when I was six or seven years old (perhaps in the *Saturday Evening Post*), and it drew me straight into the world of gunning. It was called *Whistling for Plover*, and it showed a hunter down on his knees in a flat, marshy, no-man's-land with the ghostly outlines of sailing craft—brigantines, skipjacks, schooners—coasting offshore in the background. The hunter is wearing a narrow-brimmed straw hat, a loose-sleeved white blouse buttoned tight to the throat; and angling forward expertly from beneath his right arm is a short-barreled, muzzle-loading hammer gun that looks to be about a 10-gauge, perhaps a Greener. The old painting's oils looked cracked and faded but you could still smell the damp salt breeze, the marsh muck, the sulfurous funk of burnt black powder.

The riveting thing about the painting was that the gunner was a black man, what we called in those days a Negro—dark as midnight, flat-nosed, thick-lipped—and every inch a bird hunter. His hooded eyes scan the sky warily, lips pursed to whistle the birds into range—*whew, whew, whew*—and the wicked hooks of his gun's cocked hammers spelled my kind of business. Around him lie the crumpled forms of nearly a dozen fresh-killed shorebirds—greater yellow legs, I discovered much later, which the market gunners of those days sold on city streets from Baltimore to Chicago as "Yellow-Legged Plover" for as little as half a dollar a hundred.

The sweep of the view, its eerie flatness, the dim white sails of the distant workboats, the wind-ruffled white shirt, the stark, black, brutally efficient lines of the gun, the strange intensity of the gunner's face—strange because as far as I knew at that tender age only rich old white men hunted birds—made me want to be part of that scene, or one very like it, wherever or whenever it was still happening and with whomever I might find shooting there. Since then I've found it in many places: waiting for waterfowl in the tidewater marshes of Maryland's Eastern Shore, in the birdsong-bright darkness of the African game plains, on the mudflats of the Alaskan panhandle where we bucked the dawn tides for geese, in California and Montana, Georgia and Texas, from Maine to Mexico to England, but mainly and most delightfully in my own home coverts, in Wisconsin, in New York, and finally in Vermont, seeking woodcock or ruffed grouse.

The dawning influences on my development as a writer were Edgar Rice Burroughs, Lev Nikolayevich Tolstoy, Jim Kjelgaard, Franz Kafka, and Ernest Hemingway.

The purple prose of Burroughs, whom I first read when I was nine, made me want to go to Africa, and twenty years later I got there for the first of six long safaris over the span of four decades.

The snipe shooting sequence in Tolstoy's *Anna Karenina* is the best gundog writing I've ever read. Levin is shooting near his estate with a couple of wealthy friends, Veslovsky and Oblonsky. On the second day of the shoot, Levin rises before dawn and—miffed at the ineptitude of his companions—sneaks out into the snipe marsh with his real hunting partner, his setter bitch Laska. She quickly makes game. We see this scene from the dog's point of view:

> She was struck more and more powerfully, more and more definitely, by their scent; suddenly it became perfectly clear to her that one of them was right there, behind that hummock, five steps in front of her; she halted and her whole body grew rigid. Her short legs made it impossible for her to see anything in front of her, but by the smell she could tell it was not more than five steps away. She stood there, more and more aware of its presence and enjoying the anticipation. Her rigid tail was outstretched, only its very tip twitching. Her mouth was slightly open and her ears pricked up. One of her ears had got folded back while she was running; she was breathing heavily, but cautiously, and she looked round her still more cautiously, more with her eyes than with her head, at her master. He, with his familiar face, and eyes that were always so terrifying, came stumbling over the hummocks, it seemed to her extraordinarily slowly. It appeared to her that he was walking slowly, though he was running.

Without a by-your-leave, no apologies to anyone, Tolstoy has changed points of view twice in as many paragraphs, captured the essence of a rough shoot, and shown us precisely how we must appear to our gun-dogs: big, slow, and frightening.

Jim Kjelgaard, whom I was lucky enough to meet when I was ten years old, wrote not only the Big Red series of juvenile books about Irish setters but many more with guns and game birds in them. He was a short, neat, soft-spoken, and kindly man who treated dogs and small boys with equal affection. He stood on Tolstoy's shoulders, to be sure, but he stood there firmly and in an American stance.

Of course I never met Kafka, who died in 1924, ten years before I was born, but to my mind he's one of the best writers of animal stories in all of the world's literature. Think of them: *The Metamorphosis* (man becomes cockroach), *Investigations of a Dog* (who delves into deeper things than garbage cans), *A Report to an Academy* (by a captive chimpanzee from the Gold Coast), and the best of the lot, *The Burrow*. It was one of the last long stories Kafka wrote. The narrator is a cruel, paranoid, badgerlike animal who begins to suspect that something larger, smarter, and meaner is lurking out there, beyond his warren, a "beast" waiting to crunch him—as he, the narrator, has crunched so many specimens of the lesser breeds. The story details his frantic, claustrophobic efforts to counter the "beast's" threat with ever-more-elaborate tunneling projects, mazes within mazes, until—in the final paragraph—he suddenly realizes that Death is already inside, about to take him. That beats *Lassie Come Home, The Jungle Book, My Friend Flicka*, or any one of Aesop's fables six ways from Sunday.

Ernest Hemingway, of course, is the father of us all—or at least those of us who love to hunt and fish. In an *Esquire* column of February 1935, when I was not yet a year old, he wrote of game birds:

I think they were all made to shoot because if they were not why did they give them that whirr of wings that moves you suddenly more than any love of country? Why did they make them all so good to eat. . . ? Why does the curlew have that voice, and who thought up the plover's call, which takes the place of noise of wings, to give us that catharsis wing shooting has given to men since they stopped flying hawks and took to fowling pieces? I think that they were made to shoot and some of us were made to shoot them and if that is not so well, never say we did not tell you that we liked it.

All of these influences and more are present, for better or worse, in the short stories and essays that comprise this book. Many of these pieces first appeared in *Shooting Sportsman Magazine,* and I'd like to thank its editor in chief, Silvio Calabi, for allowing me the freedom to explore whichever aspects of the subject struck my fancy. Thanks also to Ralph Stuart, editor of *SSM;* to Terry McDonell, editor in chief of *Sports Afield;* Ed Gray, former editor of *Gray's Sporting Journal;* Chris Dorsey of Ducks Unlimited; and to Doug Truax of Countrysport Press, who edited *A Breed Apart,* in which my story "Rusty & Belle" first appeared.

Finally and foremost, my gratitude to Lilly Golden, who encouraged me to pull this book together and edited it with a careful but loving eye.

Are You Lonesome Tonight?

THE ROAD RAN through yellowing woods and fields up over a hill and then dropped away toward a swale where a stock pond glinted back up at them through a dark beard of alders. He turned off to the right at a break in the stone wall and parked the truck out of sight at the top of the ridge behind a copse of young aspens. The dog danced briefly on the seat beside him, teeth clacking with happy little yips barely suppressed. They'd been here before. He let the dog out, then unzipped the sheep-lined case behind the bench seat and withdrew the gun. The dog sat shivering at his boots. He reached in and pulled out the bell collar, a musical tingle of steel that made the dog's ears twitch. He buckled the collar around the dog's thick, black neck, took two shells from his vest, broke the gun, blew down the barrels for luck, and loaded.

Hunt 'em up, Luke.

The dog lined out fast down the footpath, head up, nostrils flared, into the wind. Let him run it out quick, he thought. I could whistle him back and keep him cool, but he needs the run, let him get it out of his system, and there's nothing this close to the road anyway.

But there was. Luke spun in midstride, tail up, and dove nose first into a thicket of maple whips beside the trail. A woodcock sprang twittering skyward and flicked out, twisting on wide, high wings through the leaftops.

Gone before he got the gun halfway to his shoulder.

That'll learn ye, he thought.

Luke glared back at him balefully.

My mistake, he told the dog. *Too slow. But it's only the first of the season. Cut me some slack, why don't you?*

They worked on down an old logging road flanked by a stone wall, with a brush-grown field to their left and a steep hillside of mature shagbark hickory to the right. Luke worked the wall and the pucker-brush beside it, quartering short and quick, nose up, then down, then up again, into the wind. The logging road bent away to the right just past an old, silt-bottomed stock pond where the man paused to give Luke a chance at a drink. But the Lab wasn't thirsty yet. He was hungry only for birds.

The field dropped away to an alder bottom with a square of old apples and second-growth timber rising behind it. Antique apples, varieties grown no more for profit. A small spring-fed brook thick-edged with alders marked the break from field to covert. He called this patch the Seep Square, and over the years it had been good to them. There were two ways to hunt the Seep Square, depending on the amount of time you wanted to hunt.

If you had time enough, you could hunt it from the alder bottom up. That way any birds you flushed and missed would fly deeper into the country, and you could spend a pleasant couple of hours working the hills for reflushes.

Short of time, you could circle out to the top of the Seep Square and push it back fast toward the alder bottom. Unhit birds would not fly across the open field for fear of hawks. They would break to the left for the complex lobe of covert beyond the hickory ridge. That hunt took less than an hour, and was always good for at least a couple of woodcock. But the longer hunt meant more time behind the dog, more time pounding the woods, and held in the thornapples the promise of grouse. It was a luxury.

To hell with time, he thought.

The seep itself was muck-bottomed and tall with ripening cattails and they waded through to the other side, where he called Luke to heel. He knelt beside the dog on dry ground at the edge of the alders and put his arm around the dog's neck. *Take it slow and easy through here. Work it good. They hold tight this early in the season, most of 'em will. They haven't been hunted yet. All right?*

All right, hunt 'em up.

He dropped down off a weathered boulder into the thick of it, weaving and ducking behind the quartering dog, stepping high over the canted trunks of dying alders, pushing others aside with his gloved foreend hand. The alders cracked like rotten bones. It was dark in here, fetid, windless, with charlie behind the eyeballs, an RPG at the ready. He held the light 20-gauge double upright with his bare trigger hand, angled forward the better to mount it quickly at a flush, moving fast but with his eyes on the dog, alert to any sudden sound or a sudden brightening of Luke's color. Luke always lit up like black neon when he marked a bird, and his flailing feathered tail always shot upright, beating like a metronome gone mad.

It was a familiar tail, a recognized rhythm.

About twenty steps into the alders, Luke cut quickly up toward the dry ground, lighting up, and a woodcock got up, rising loud as pennywhistles up toward the sunlight, and he caught it square at the top of its rise as it hit the light, a russet flash, unconscious of even mounting the gun, and popped the bird down in a puff of tiny, dark-eyed, slowly falling feathers. The alders ate the sound of the shot.

Luke picked up the woodcock and brought it over. The man took it from his easy jaws. A bead of blood glistened at the tip of the long, odd beak, and the big eyes were closed. Dead before it hit the ground. *Good work, man. First of the year. Nines do the job, don't they?* He let Luke sniff the blood and suck in the rich, hot, dry mud scent of woodcock fresh dead. Maybe I shouldn't do that, he thought; some say it floods a dog's nose against the scent of the next bird. But Luke loves it so, and it's a luxury anyway. Why shouldn't a dog have a luxury? Then he had a sniff himself. He pocketed the bird, feeling it warm inside the canvas against the small of his back.

Okay, he said. *Hunt 'em up.*

They pushed on down through the rest of the alder brake with no more flushes and cut right along a tumbling stone wall toward the top of the Seep Square. Luke worked the wall thoroughly and cut back across the track of the gun to frisk the interior thickets. They came to the first of the old apple trees, Luke looking back toward the man to make sure he was close enough before he went in on it. A grouse got up with a roar from under the apple tree, boring out low and straight with the tree trunk obscuring the shot, then soared high out of range toward the top of the thornapple rise, tilting, sunlight gleaming silver-stained across his wings and back.

Luke looked over again, pained at the gun's silence.

Yes, the man said, nodding mock gravely. *They'll do that, you know. All the naive birds in these parts were killed off two centuries ago. Only the smart survive.*

He squinted up at the sun, then checked his watch. Twenty minutes from the truck, three flushes, one woodcock in pocket. One woodcock makes mighty thin soup.

Hunt 'em up.

They crossed the far stone wall that marked the top of the Seep Square and cut left again and began to sinuate their way up through the thornapples. Luke picked his steps carefully from bush to bush with memories of those bitterly hooked thorns of yore buried stem-deep in his pads. The man now carried a tweezers in his game vest against that possibility. The first time it happened, ten years ago when they were new to this country, he pulled the thorn out of Luke's paw with his teeth. Such an experience gets a person close to his dog in a hurry.

Halfway up the slope Luke got birdy. He put his nose up, inhaled, then ran fast to his left up and across while the man jumped clear of the thornapples into the open sunlight and a grouse got up, flushing back downhill like thunder toward the man, just over his head; and he spun on his heel, mounting the gun, and caught the bird going away as it poured downhill. He centered it, *pow*, and watched it spin sideways, corkscrewing ass over tip in a long, hard, crazy fall back down toward the bottom of the thornapples. *Thump*, dead, in a splash of feathers. Luke was past him, disappearing into the brush. No one runs on Luke.

The man waited, confident. He heard scrabbling in the leaves below, then the dog emerged from the brush and came wagging slowly uphill, his whole body wagging, with that shy, self-deprecating look they have when they've done it well, grinning around a mouthful of big, dead, head-lolling grouse body, one wing dangling alop.

He sat on the hillside, the gun broken open by his side in the short, dry grass, and took the grouse from Luke's mouth and spread its fan. A bird of the year by its heft, a hen bird by the mottled break in the center of the glossy blue-black tail bar. He lay the bird in his lap and opened the Buck knife, felt around for its crop, slit the neck, and extracted the crop. It felt full and lumpy. He slit the tough, pawky integument of the crop and squeezed its contents into his palm. Chunks of yellow-fleshed, red-skinned thornapple, a few dark green leaves, a catkin or two, probably birch by their color.

A cooling breeze worked back up the slope and he took off his cap to let his brow dry. He pulled out a pack of cigarettes. Luke lay panting by his side, squinting against the sunlight. He lay his free hand on the dog's wide, silken brow and ran it slowly down the heavy-muscled neck, working his fingers deep into the coarse black hairs of Luke's ruff. There was blood on the back of his hand, his own blood, welling slowly to the previous kiss of the briers. The cuts stung faintly, astringent, no worse than the tingle of aftershave.

The dog looked up and raised an eyebrow. He thumped his tail.

The valley spread out below them, yellow and green and red, the big sugar maples ballooning their crowns to the sky. The town lay strung like a necklace of sugar cubes along the winding dirt road, and to the east a church spire offered its impudent finger to heaven. Next to the spire he could see the graveyard, its moss-blackened stones just visible from this height of land. One of the tombstones, he knew, bore a timeworn legend.

ELIZABETH HARDWEAL
May 26, 1798–December 23, 1822
In the 25th Year of Her Age
"She Come to Town on a Viset"

Beyond the valley rose another range of mountains, Shatterack and Bear and Moffat and Equinox most prominent among them, and on the dim-hazed horizon the blue-black rim of the Greens themselves.

He pictures her coming to town for the Christmas season, to visit relatives, probably from Massachusetts or Connecticut where they all came from in those days. What was it? Diphtheria? Fever? The bloody flux? Was she pretty? He hopes so. Perhaps they had partridge for supper before she fell ill. Maybe she went through the ice one night, skating.

God how he loves her. . . .

Are you lonesome tonight?

Well, we all come to town on a viset.

They breathed the sweet fall air, man and dog, in love now with the whole whistling world. The man stood stiffly and pocketed the grouse. Its weight and warmth felt comfortable against the small of his back, more than balancing that of the cooling woodcock. He stooped and picked up the shotgun, reloaded it, and clicked it shut with that sweet sound of a bank vault closing.

There's two more birds still down there, he told the dog, *a big one and a little one. Or at least that we know of.*

Hunt 'em up.

RUSTY & BELLE

In the best of all possible worlds, a boy should start hunting with his father, or perhaps with a kindly uncle. But my dad, though he was a keen angler, didn't care much for the shooting sports, and my only hunting uncle happened to be in jail during my formative years. (That's another story.) So my education as a budding Nimrod took a different course. In fact, like Mowgli in Kipling's *The Jungle Book*, I was taught how to hunt by the wolves.

Well, okay . . . so maybe they weren't wolves, exactly. But a brace of half-wild, hell-for-leather Irish setters is probably the next best thing. How Rusty and Belle sniffed me out as a candidate for on-the-job training, I really don't know. I never even knew who actually owned them.

And yet, during a single glorious, murderous, never-to-be-forgotten autumn just after World War II, I found myself hunting behind them, gradually learning the nuances of the chase, gunning my first game birds over them, and developing under their rude tutelage a lifelong love of upland shooting. First times, as they say, are always the best.

Ever since my family had moved, in the fall of 1941, to the far western reaches of Wauwatosa in southern Wisconsin, I'd been mesmerized by game birds. Across the road from our newly built home lay a broad belt of virgin tallgrass prairie, stretching nearly a mile down to the Menomonee River. That reach of the Upper Middle West is part of what scientists call the Prairie Peninsula, islands of grassland studded across the great, dark green sea of the northern forests. This configuration provides lots of "edge," and the region was therefore rich in wildlife. Bison had roamed these prairie islands, as far east as Pennsylvania and New York, but the last of Wisconsin's buffalo was killed in 1832. Game birds remained abundant, though. Ruffed grouse, sharptails and prairie chickens, woodcock and snipe, clouds of ducks, and later the newly introduced ringneck pheasant—all proliferated on or around these grassy islands. In that time and place, it was almost inevitable that a boy should become an upland hunter.

That first winter in the new house, I began noticing clusters of large, brown, football-shaped birds scuttling around in the field across the road as they fed in the snow on grass seed knocked down by the wind. I was not yet seven years old, but something ignited in my heart. I wanted to hold one in my hands, maybe study its feathers up close, perhaps even pluck them out—though I knew the bird would have to be dead for me to do that. Okay, so I'd kill it first. And then when it was plucked . . .

And then what?

I'd eat it!

Yes, hunting is instinctive with us, despite the arguments of the antis. *I had to have one of those birds.*

"What are they, Dad?" I asked one afternoon as my father and I were shoveling snow in front of the house. He looked across the street. A dozen of the big birds were feeding busily in the field near the road.

"Prairie chickens," he said.

I stared longingly at them, less than a hundred feet away.

"They don't make good pets," he said.

"I don't want one as a pet," I said. "I want to kill one. We could cook it up for supper tonight."

He laughed.

"Don't let your mother hear you say that," he said. My mother was a sentimentalist, weeping quietly whenever a songbird snuffed itself against a storm window, or at the mere thought of a dead raccoon on the road.

One of the birds was feeding toward us, well away from the rest of the flock. "See if you can hit him with a snowball," my dad said.

I packed a good one, small and heavy and tight and round as I could make it. I crossed the road directly toward the bird. Not even looking up, he scurried back to the flock. I kept going. With every step I gained on them, they edged away deeper into the wind-bent grass. I couldn't get within range this way. I sprinted toward them in nightmare slow motion, the metal clasps of my heavy galoshes rattling as I ran. They scuttled a bit faster. Finally, panting, I hurled the snowball. They avoided it with ease and kept on feeding. By the time I'd had enough, I was a quarter of a mile into the prairie, knee-deep in snow, red-faced and slick with sweat, and my arm ached from futile throws at unhittable targets. I plodded back to my father, who was gentleman enough to hide the grin that was threatening to erupt into a boy-shattering guffaw.

"A snowball's no good," I said.

"Guess not."

"Dad, could I have a bow and some arrows?"

"We'll see," he said.

For Christmas that year I received a lemonwood longbow of fifteen pounds' pull. I was a big kid for my age, but the bow was too strong for me at first. I persevered, shooting at snowmen in the backyard during the winter, or hay bales or bushelbaskets or (when the grown-ups weren't looking) the occasional pumpkin in the neighborhood's communal Victory Garden across the road the following summer; and by fall I felt I was ready. I wasn't. Oh, sure, I could shoot a Pound Sweet apple out of the neighbor's backyard tree, and once I grazed a fat robin tugging a worm from the earth after a rainstorm, but I couldn't hit a prairie chicken that first autumn to save my wretched soul. I lost arrow after arrow, shooting at birds on the ground, and never nicked a one. They dodged the arrows as readily as they had my first snowball, and the arrows inevitably slithered off beneath the matted grass, rarely to fly again.

I began making my own arrows out of the long pinewood dowels my mom used to support leggy garden plants, fletching them with brightly dyed turkey feathers from a cheap Indian warbonnet that one of my aunts had given me for my eighth birthday. In hopes of saving arrows, I arrived independently at the principle of the flu-flu, in which the fletching is glued around the tail of the shaft in corkscrew fashion to slow down the final flight of the arrow, and learned how to stalk in quite close to the flock before shooting—sometimes as close as thirty feet.

Finally I hit a prairie chicken, a young one, just as the flock was rising in panic from my best stalk ever. I broke her wing, and it took me half an hour of frantic chasing through tangles of the low-lying sawgrass we called "ripgut" before I finally batted her flat with the bow. I fell on her like a fumbled football and wrung her rubbery neck.

I sat there in the prairie, with the bluestem towering over my head, my hands and bare forearms stinging from sweat and innumerable grass cuts, with hard, sharp grass seeds stuck in the blood that seeped from the slashes, holding her at last in my hands. She was hot, dusty smelling, heavy, limp, and dead as a doornail. I ruffled the transverse chocolate-and-white bars on her breast again and again, as I later would the short, thick, soft hair of the first girl I ever loved. Never in my life had I been happier than I was at that moment.

But I knew there had to be a better way.

That way was with a dog and a gun.

My grandfather, Frank Jones, had led a peripatetic life as a young man, before the turn of the twentieth century. Born in 1871, he'd run away from home in Chicago at the age of fourteen after smashing a slate over a schoolmaster's head when that man falsely accused him of whispering to a classmate. He'd bummed around the Midwest, working on farms, becoming a dab hand with horse teams. He drifted into the small towns occasionally, working as a shop clerk, a hackney driver, and, once, an assistant to an undertaker, among other odd jobs, but finally fetching up back in Chicago. There he became a foreman on the production line in a packing house. The company he worked for, maybe it was Swift or Armour, I can't remember, had developed a revolutionary new canning process, and a New York City packer pirated him away to steal the new technique. He went to New York in 1890 and remained there for nearly ten years. When his boss at the packing plant told him that all employees would be expected to vote for the Republican incumbent, Benjamin Harrison, over Grover Cleveland in the upcoming 1892 presidential election, my grandfather quit his job, though he was still a few months shy of twenty-one and couldn't have voted if he'd wanted to. He was damned if anyone would tell him how to vote.

Out of work, he and an unemployed partner pooled their resources, bought an old breech-loading 12-bore W. W. Greener hammer gun, rented a team and a buckboard, and went across the Hudson River to the Jersey Palisades to hunt for the New York restaurant market. They brought along a stray dog they'd befriended, a lop-eared, curly-coated, liver-colored pooch named Fred who may have been an American water spaniel.

"I didn't care what breed he was," my grandfather used to say. "Old Fred was good at his job and that's all I cared about."

"What did you hunt for?" I asked him.

"Mud bats, pa'tridges, and prairie hens," he told me. I later deciphered those names to mean woodcock, ruffed grouse, and—of all things—heath hens, the last-named being the eastern equivalent of my beloved greater prairie chicken (*Tympanuchus cupido*). The heath hen died out in the early years of this century, almost simultaneously with the last of the passenger pigeons that once darkened the skies of nineteenth-century America during their spring and fall migrations, both birds the victims of unbridled habitat destruction and wanton American bloodlust.

But while it lasted, the hunting was superb, too easy the way my granddad told it. One of them would drive the wagon through the little pockets of open country back of the Palisades while the other walked ahead, with the dog and the gun, popping whatever got up. "We'd cross the river on a Friday night and come back Monday morning with the spring wagon groaning. We got two bits apiece for the bigger birds, and a nickel each for the little fellas."

To me, at the age of ten, it sounded like heaven on earth.

"Do you still have that shotgun?" I asked hopefully.

"No," my granddad said, rolling another cigarette. He was a lean, leathery old man already in his seventies, with hard gray eyes, a thin scar of a mouth, nicotine-stained fingers, and a great, gritty fund of stories. He would live to be eighty-seven and to rise up from his deathbed on the final morning of his life to shave himself with his cutthroat straight razor, having reshingled his roof, unaided, only a few weeks before. "And even if I did still have that old iron," he added, "I'd dassent give it to you. Your ma would never forgive me."

Clearly I would have to seek elsewhere for a shotgun, and when I found it, keep any knowledge of the gun or of my hunting adventures from my tender-hearted, gun-hating mother. The few birds and rabbits I'd killed so far with the bow, I'd cooked and eaten out in the fields where I shot them. My friends and I filched lard, salt, and matches from home, a little bit at a time, and kept them hidden in a "fort" we had dug on the prairie. We dug it into a sidehill, roofed it over with scrap lumber we swiped from a nearby building project (already the prairie was being nibbled to death by postwar housing development), and laid thick slabs of bluestem sod over the boards. We salvaged a rusty old frying pan from the town dump, cleaned it up with bootlegged Brillo pads, added an old-fashioned stoneware coffeepot one of the gang found in his attic, hauled water-smoothed rocks up from the river to build a fireplace, and were snug as jolly plainsmen in our splendid hideaway. It had everything a boy could desire—including a huge stack of moldy comic books. Everything but a gun and a couple of bird dogs.

Enter Rusty and Belle.

They came trotting up to the hidden entrance of our our fort one hot September Saturday when a couple of us were boiling some crayfish we'd caught in the river. Crayfish were called "crabs" in those parts, and they were a pretty big subspecies, some of them six or eight inches long. We caught them with a hunk of liver tied to a piece of butcher's string and dangled near their holes in the shallows, under the river rocks. You let them glom on, hoisted them gently up near the top of the water, then netted them with your baseball cap. We boiled them up in an old Maxwell House coffee can after letting them soak for about an hour or so in clear, cold water to clean the mud out of their systems. When they were done, they turned red as lobsters. We cracked them open with stones, sprinkled salt on the pieces, and ate them, sometimes with Saltines and peanut butter for dessert.

Snuffle, snuffle, snuffle. We saw two big, square, wet noses poking into the doorway. Nostrils big as gun muzzles, flexing open and shut as they sniffed the delicious smells.

"Cripes, it's a couple of dogs."

"I know them," Danny said. "They're Rusty and Belle. I think they're called Irish setters."

My ears perked up. A setter was a hunting dog. I'd never seen the Irish variety, though.

"Hand me my bow and quiver," I said.

"You're not gonna shoot 'em, are you?"

"No, asshole. I'm gonna see if they know how to hunt."

I brought out some crabmeat and a handful of Saltines for the dogs. They accepted the snacks eagerly and looked up for more.

"You've got to earn it," I told them. I strung the bow (I'd graduated to a thirty-five-pound Osage orange longbow by this time), nocked a homemade flu-flu arrow, and headed off at a trot toward where I'd seen a small family group of prairie chickens only about an hour before.

We were hunting into the wind, so the bird scent would blow back down to the dogs. The only trouble was that they stayed right at my heels. No good, I thought. I want them out in front. I stopped. Rusty stopped too, and looked up at me. His eyes held the big question.

"Go ahead," I said, gesturing with my free hand. "Hunt 'em up!"

Belle responded first to my command, suddenly lighting out and hunting forward on a zigzag line with her head high, sucking in the hot autumn wind. Rusty took off after her, quartering in counterpoint to her course. Whenever they got more than fifteen yards ahead of me, I whistled them back, then sent them out again. I don't believe they'd ever been trained to this, but they must have had at least a smidgen of hunting instinct left, though I've read since that the breed had gone almost exclusively to bench stock by then. The red gods were certainly feeling benevolent that day, to send me by sheerest chance these eager, alert, glossy-red bird dogs.

Suddenly Belle stopped. Her broad-feathered tail went up. Her head poised flat and rock-steady, almost snakelike, angling slightly downward and ahead of her. By God, she was on point!

Foolishly, I ran in ahead of her in my eagerness, and the whole flock of chickens erupted at once, a great rattling blur of brown and white. I snapped an arrow after them but missed miserably. The birds flew on, fast and low, a few strong wingbeats, then a long gliding pause, then a few more wingbeats, until they were just dots at the far end of the prairie.

I could barely bring myself to look at Belle, whom I was sure must be furious at me for blowing the shot. But she wasn't. She looked delighted with herself, smirking and pirouetting like a wanton minx. She and Rusty hunted on. We pushed through the tall, golden grass toward where the birds had pitched in.

About halfway there, Belle pointed again. This time I kept my head, walking in slowly ahead of her with the arrow nocked firmly and the bow held crosswise at waist height. A large, long-tailed bird suddenly scuttled ahead a few steps and took wing. A pheasant! A big, slow, green-headed, white-necked, bronze-gleaming cockbird, cackling metallically as he lifted off. I drew, fired, and hit him, and he tumbled end for end into the grass as feathers drifted off downwind. Rusty, who had been to one side, was on him like a flash. I ran up quickly, not knowing if Rusty would run off with the bird to eat it, and while he was still wrestling with it got it away from him and wrung its neck. I praised both dogs to the skies and they wagged their tails in delight. It was my first ringneck ever, and only a lucky hit at the base of the left wing accounted for our bagging it. On the way back to the fort, Belle jumped a rabbit, which I also managed to kill. A great day! I rewarded my newfound friends with a fair share of the rabbit meat when we fried it up that afternoon in our underground hideaway.

Later that fall, I arranged to buy a beat-up old single-barreled, 28-gauge Savage Model 220 from a kid in my grade at school. The gun was choked improved-cylinder and had a 28-inch barrel. Ron's dad was a wealthy doctor who spoiled his son rotten, and had just bought him a 16-gauge "Eagle Grade" L. C. Smith. I gave Ron eight dollars for the Savage—money I'd been paid by neighbors for mowing lawns and shoveling snow, hard-earned every penny of it. Ron threw in three boxes of low-base 7 1/2s and one of high-brass 6s, along with a can of Hoppe's nitro solvent and a cleaning rod. No contemporary gun deal in the streets of Miami or Harlem ever went down more surreptitiously.

I couldn't bring the gun home for fear my parents would discover it—my mom was an inveterate snoop, always poking around in my room while I was at school to see what I'd been up to. So I wrapped the Savage in oily rags and kept it, during the week, in the fort. That didn't work for long, though. Every minute of every day, I was afraid some tramp would wander up from the Milwaukee Road right-of-way just across the river and find the fort. He'd swipe my gun and hold up a bank, or something. It was driving me nuts. My schoolwork also suffered.

I had a friend named Harry who lived near the grade school, and I prevailed on him to let me hide the shotgun in his garage. There were fields across the road from the school, just like the ones across from my house, and I figured to do some hunting there after school, or on the weekends. Rusty and Belle had taken to following me to school that fall, hanging out in the playground during class hours and playing "keep away" with us during recess or the noon hour. Once they saw, smelled, and heard the gun go off, they were even more strongly bonded to me. I've often wondered what their rightful owners thought they were up to during those long, long absences from home.

It took a lot of trial and error—more of the latter than the former —to perfect a decent shooting style with the Savage. But my experience in wingshooting with the bow stood me in good stead. The bow had taught me how to swing with a rising bird, and keep swinging as I released the shot. With the shotgun, I had a tendency to overlead birds—especially rising woodcock, which have a disconcerting habit of pausing at the top of the rise before zigzagging out on the level through the tops of a covert. Pheasants were easy, though—slow, loud, straight-away fliers. Ruffed grouse were harder, startling me to the point of paralysis in the racket they made getting up, then lining out low or with a tree between them and the gun, denying me a shot either way.

I wouldn't shoot at a really low bird for fear of hitting one of the dogs. I also swore off rabbits for the same reason. I could never break Rusty and Belle of tear-assing off after every bunny they jumped, like greyhounds at a dog-track. Once, Belle ran a bunny into a long piece of drainage pipe, wide enough for the rabbit but not for the dog. Rusty fig-ured out instantly what was happening and leaped to the far end of the pipe, just in time to intercept the panicky rabbit when it emerged a moment later, still at full gallop. The gluttonous mutts quickly ripped it apart and ate it. I figured this must have been the way they hunted before they took up with me. Old habits die hard.

No, they weren't perfect gundogs by any means. In addition to eat-ing perhaps one in every five birds I killed, they had a tendency to take off suddenly for parts unknown in the middle of a hunt, sometimes not returning until the next day. Rusty was a car chaser, and Belle a cat chaser. They inevitably took on any skunk they happened across, with predictably malodorous results. Fortunately we lived too far south for porcupines. Once they tackled a big boar raccoon, though, and before they learned their lesson both of them had deep gashes in their noses, flanks, and bellies that put them out of action for the better part of a week.

But now and then they were splendid. I'll never forget a double point that occurred one November afternoon in the fields across the railroad tracks. We'd been puddle-jumping mallards along the river, with only sporadic success, when Belle—who had the better nose—suddenly lit up. I followed her into the wind, away from the river, across the tracks, and into a low, damp swale that gave way to cattails before rising again to a farmer's planting of field corn. At the edge of the swale she froze on point. Rusty pussyfooted up behind her, then looked to his left. Sniffed a couple times. He angled over in that direction about ten yards and locked up.

Could be the same bird, I thought. A runner, moving ahead of Belle's point. But when I went in ahead of Belle, a woodcock got up right under her nose. As I mounted the gun, I heard and then saw from the corner of my eye a big cock pheasant vault skyward from Rusty's point—no doubt flushed by the piping of the woodcock's wing feathers. It was one of those bright, cold, cobalt blue Wisconsin afternoons—no wind, sunlight gleaming on the dogs' rich mahogany-colored fur, the field corn pale yellow in the background, the cock pheasant resplendent in full flight.

"I'll kill 'em both!" I thought as the flight paths of woodcock and ringneck momentarily crossed. I shot in that instant. Both birds fell.

That's gunning at its best.

Rusty and Belle disappeared from my life that winter with the arrival of the first deep snows, which put an end to the bird shooting. I have no idea what became of them. Maybe their owner moved away. Maybe they died—both of them were reckless enough. Whatever it was, though, I'm sure it had nothing to do with a loss of interest in hunting. I've rarely met a keener pair of gundogs, nonstop indefatigable. I'll always be grateful to them for infecting me with that enthusiasm when it counted most.

My mother never learned of Rusty and Belle—not until I told her about them, years later, toward the end of her life.

"Where did you develop this unhealthy passion for blood sports?" she asked me one afternoon when I was visiting from my home in the East. "You never got it from me or your father."

I told her the story, just about the way I've told it here. Her eyes began to fill with tears.

"If I'd known it meant so much to you, I would have allowed you to hunt," she said. "Better that than keep it *hidden* from me all those years."

Suddenly I was sorry I'd confessed. But then I looked out the front window, across the street. It was wall-to-wall suburbia now, clear down to the river. Not an acre of native prairie left. Fat chance, I thought. Don't feel sorry for her, feel sorry for what's gone. She just doesn't get it. None of them do. They never will.

TWO TRAMPS IN MUD-TIME

Kids have always been bloodthirsty, boys especially —pint-sized cavemen at heart, only too eager to hunt or make war. In my own boyhood experience, the line between those activities was blurred to indistinction. It took a near-tragic incident on a wet, dark, muddy November morning nearly half a century ago to show me the difference.

I'd been jump-shooting ducks that season, with my single-shot 28-gauge Savage Model 220, along a river that ran near my home. Mallards mostly, with now and then a shoveller or a teal; and when I dumped them in the river, they were quickly swept downstream on boisterous brown currents swelled by the autumn rains. I didn't have a retriever of my own in those days, just a neighbor's pair of half-wild Irish setters, Rusty and Belle. They were fine on upland birds but worthless on waterfowl. Belle didn't like getting wet, and though Rusty would go quite gaily into the river to pick up my fallen ducks, he'd then—with a twinkle in his eyes—swim across to the other side and eat them.

So I usually left the setters behind when I went for ducks. If the birds fell on land, all was well. But usually they dropped in the river, and then it was catch-as-catch-can. While the dead or wounded whirled downstream, I chased along the banks, hoping they'd be swept ashore or hang up on a convenient snag where I could wade out to them. More often than not, though, they'd outrace me on those swift currents. Even in death they deftly avoided the swamped willows and driftwood shoals that grasped for them. Nothing is sadder than watching a moribund greenhead swirl downstream on its back, faster than a boy can run, its orange paddles waving farewell to the sky.

Then I read a piece in an outdoor magazine—maybe it was in "Tap's Tips"—that promised a solution to my problem. The article suggested carrying the butt section and reel of a bait-casting rod along on a retrieverless duck hunt. When a duck was down on the water you could simply cast just beyond it with a floating plug, hook it by the body or a wing, and reel it in.

More easily said than done. Growing up as an angler on Wisconsin's vaunted muskie, pike, and bass lakes, I could cast a plug fairly accurately even at the age of twelve. But only at stationary targets— the lily pads, sawlogs, and weed beds under which game fish lurked. A dead duck whisking downstream at speeds of up to ten miles an hour, dancing and twirling and bobbing like a crazed balletomane, was another matter. I snagged a few of them but it still wasn't good enough.

Then I thought of stillwater and the prairie potholes. When the soaking rains of November arrived, the clay-pocketed low spots on the grasslands just west of town always filled for a few weeks, providing convenient way stations for southbound ducks. The puddles grew to small ponds, rarely more than a hundred feet across, tucked away in folded swells grown round with big bluestem, switchgrass, foxtail barley, and prairie cordgrass—great ambush cover. It was merely a question of which particular pond the ducks might be using on a given day. And there were dozens, maybe hundreds of them in the stretch of prairie I hunted.

I always enjoyed stalking those ponds, even when they drew blank. World War II was still fresh in the memory of every boy, and indeed the greatest disappointment in my young life was that it hadn't lasted long enough for me to fight in it. Stalking the ponds, I'd play infantryman—wriggling up a damp, grassy slope on my belly, shotgun cradled across my couched elbows, letting my imagination transmute the single-shot Savage into a tommy gun or a Browning Automatic Rifle while at the same time conjuring up a platoon of vile Krauts or Nips on the far side, completely oblivious to my silent approach. As I neared the top, my heart hammered. I'd peer stealthily through the tall grass, eyes slitted murderously, then leap to my feet, gun in hand. If there were no ducks on the pond that day, I'd make machine-gun noises, spraying the enemy mercilessly—*bambambambam!*—and watch them spin and fall, throwing their hands in the air as they died with curses on their wicked lips.

Gottverdammter Schweinhund of a Yankee! Eeeeyai! Arghhh!

Bambambambam! Take that, you evil bastards!

If there were a duck or two on the pond, they'd jump skyward at sight of me in a feathery burst of spray. No histrionics then. I'd swing upward through the rise, concentrate on one of them—the drake if possible—and . . . *Pop!* Sometimes a bird fell. I'd pull the truncated rod from my knapsack, tie on a plug, and start casting. . . .

The prairie ponds I hunted lay west of the river, across the railroad right-of-way, a freight route bound for the Pacific Northwest. There were still "knights of the road" in those days—bums, tramps, hoboes, vags, or bindlestiffs—jobless, homeless down-and-outers who rode the rails as freely as migrating waterfowl on the north winds of autumn. They camped out in hobo jungles, raided chicken coops, swiped pies that were cooling on kitchen windowsills, and engaged in suchlike comic-book nonsense. All kids were warned by their parents and teachers to steer clear of such good-for-nothings. All boys yearned to join them.

I got my chance that November morning.

It was a great day for ducks—windy, rainy, the sky a lowering gray that leered down on the prairie potholes like a rapist peeking through a grimy skylight. Teal had passed through by then but the mallards were trading back and forth with wild abandon. Their strong wings winnowed the darkness as I hiked to the ponds that morning through wet, rain-flattened grass. I nearly tripped on the railroad tracks. Then the sullen glare of a campfire caught my eye from the hobo jungle half a mile upstream of where I'd forded the river, but I paid it no heed.

When I got to the first pond it was still too dark to see the birds, though I could hear their wings ripping the air as they passed and circled. Later I could hear them splash down. The gabble of duck talk strengthened with the dawn. I settled in the tall weeds and waited. When it got light enough to shoot, I stood and waited some more until the birds spotted me. A knotted raft of them rose in a great wet whir. I dropped one on the rise—a hen, as it turned out; I still couldn't distinguish color—and reloaded quickly while the stragglers got the message. I'd been trying to perfect a technique I'd read about in some of my books on Africa in which an elephant hunter with a double rifle holds two cartridges between the fingers of his fore-end hand, then breaks the rifle after he's emptied it and silently sticks in the reloads. It worked. Try it sometime. I got a second bird at long range as it trailed on out from the initial flush—a drake, dead when he hit the water.

As always I left the ducks floating in hopes that they'd serve as decoys. A few minutes later another flight swept by, circled the pond, circled again, lower this time, then cupped in with confidence. I dropped one, missed the second. This was starting to be fun.

By midmorning I had half a dozen birds dead on the water, five of them drakes. But I was down to the last four rounds in the box I'd brought with me. It was then that Willie and Joe appeared.

They came up the grassy rise behind me in total silence, thanks to the wet grass, and paused at the crest. What caused me to turn around I still don't know—maybe a muffled cough, maybe just the weight of their eyes on my back. The first thing I thought of when I saw them was Bill Mauldin's GIs, Willie and Joe, in the World War II newspaper cartoons, replete with scraggly half-grown beards and tattered cloth-ing—war-surplus army fatigues and khaki wool helmet-liners for caps. But these guys looked ominous.

They'd stopped about twenty yards away.

"We heard you shooting," one of them said. His voice was hoarse, as if there were scabs on his tonsils.

"What kind of gun is that?" the other guy asked. He smiled sweetly. His eyes were ice blue and kind of wacky looking.

"A Savage," I told him. Then hurriedly lied—"It's a repeater."

They both chuckled.

"Looks like a single-shot to me," Willie said.

"We've been in the army," Joe said. "First Division—the Big Red One. Toward the end there, when we got across the Rhine, there were Kraut kids no bigger than you fighting us. A lot of 'em carried single-shot guns like that."

"We took 'em away," said Willie. "One way or the other."

Again they chuckled, remembering.

"Let's have a look at it," Willie said. He took a step toward me with his hand outstretched for the gun. "What kind of loads you shooting?"

I raised the muzzle of the Savage in his direction. He stopped.

"Fours," I said. "High brass, copper-plated. They do the job."

"Hey, come on, kid," said Joe in a wheedling tone. "We just want to look at your gun. What's the harm in that? We're gun experts. Yeah. We're touring the country looking to buy up some prewar high-quality firearms. We might be able to offer you a good price if that piece is any good."

Willie took a step sideways, then another, dipping his off shoulder and slip-sliding like a ballroom dancer, still grinning clownishly, but separat-ing himself from Joe beyond the spread of the pattern. All the unheeded parental warnings about tramps came flooding back to me. Mainly the warnings of buggery. No longer had I any desire to join the noble ranks of the knights of the road. All I wanted was my mommy. . . .

My back was to the pond—no chance of retreat. If they made a move on me now, I'd need two shots to stop them. Two shots from a single-shot Savage. But I had a backup cartridge locked tight between the fingers of my left hand. That hand was sweating despite the cold. So was the rest of me. I knew I could reload fast. But would it be fast enough?

I suddenly realized that I didn't want to shoot.

Both men took a step toward me, grinning viciously now.

At that moment, thank God, two late-morning mallards blew low over the pond. I caught their rapid wingbeats from the corner of my eye. Without thinking I raised the gun and swung on the leader. *Pow!* It tumbled and smacked the ground, bouncing just at Willie's feet. I broke the gun quicker than ever before, no fumbling, inserted the fresh round, snapped the breech shut, and took the trailer going away, firing only a few feet over his head.

Willie yelped, "Incoming!"—and flopped flat in the mud, covering his head with his hands.

It had been a long, lucky shot, and I saw the bird fold.

I pulled out my last two loads and slipped one in, holding the other in ready reserve.

Joe stood locked in place, shivering slightly in his flap-toed combat boots.

We stared at each other.

"You're quick," he sighed. "Too quick for me." He shook his head, then looked down at his partner.

"Come on, Herb," he said, leaning over to help that combat-fatigued worthy to his feet. "We'd better get back to camp."

I pulled the plug rod from my knapsack and tied on a Jitterbug, ready to retrieve the birds that were on the pond.

Suddenly I felt relieved and generous.

"You guys must be hungry," I said. "Why don't you take those last two birds? They'll make you a hearty meal."

GLORIOUS CARNAGE

The sad thing about living through a Golden Age is that you don't appreciate it while it's happening. The label is only applied later, when whatever art or craft or wonder the age apotheosized has turned to lead.

By all accounts, the heyday of pheasant hunting in North America took place during the decade right after World War II, when I was in my teens. The birds had been thriving in the heart of the continent since the early twentieth century, enjoying the largesse of that great but already-doomed American institution, the family farm. With its woodlots and weedy edges, its corn and grain fields, its fallow ground grown tall in native grasses and seed-bearing forbs, its swamps and marshes and low soggy places as yet undrained and thus still unplowed, the family farm was approximately Pheasant Heaven. There the long-tailed birds could feed heartily, roost quietly, hide from their natural enemies when danger threatened, and raise their broods in relative peace. Egg-weakening pesticides were not yet in widespread use, and harvesting techniques were cruder than they are today, so that enough corn, wheat, barley, or rye was left on the ground after the combines went through for plenty of birds to survive even the harshest of winters.

The war itself had given pheasant populations a boost. The younger men who normally hunted them hardest each fall were off somewhere in military service. Gas and tire rationing and the scarcity of shotgun shells kept all but the keenest of the remaining gunners out of the pheasant fields and cast a cloak of peace over the midwestern countryside. In 1945, the pheasant population of North and South Dakota alone was close to thirty million. Today the whole U.S. probably contains no more than that number of the birds.

I started hunting during that prelapsarian age of abundance, but of course I was unaware of the unique opportunities it offered. Growing up in southern Wisconsin, I was not all that far—maybe six hundred miles, at best twelve hours of two-lane blacktop and Burma Shave signs in those days before the interstates—from the epicenter of the pheasant quake: Sioux Falls, South Dakota. As soon as I was old enough to drive, I should have begged, borrowed, or hot-wired a car, bidden sayonara to my kinfolk, and headed west to the Dakotas with naught but my dog and my gun. Yet I only went there once to hunt. A classmate and hunting buddy of mine was the son of a wealthy businessman who had standing invitations to hunt the big spreads northwest of Sioux Falls every fall, and in 1948, Jack and I went with him.

It was my first trip away from home without my parents, and there must have been a thousand heady new sights, sounds, smells, and ideas that impressed me as much as the hunting itself. But now all that remains in my fading memory is *The Clouds*. . . .

Yes, that's just what they were—whole cloudbanks of birds getting up from the cornrows after each drive, getting up all at once with a hell of a racket, a rattling, cackling, metallic rush of sound, a tornadic roar compounded as much of primary feathers thrashing against dry corn- stalks as it was of irate birds screaming; big explosions of color sepa- rating and lifting like giant flakes from the yellow-green background of standing corn—*bronze/red/green/white/dun*-colored splashes enclosed in swirls of wing-fanned dust—and over it all the thumps of big-bore shotguns, ragged at first but blending finally into a steady crescendo. The same sounds came from cornfields all around us, as far as the ear could hear. I remember thinking later that this was what the Civil War must have sounded like during big battles—Chickamauga or Chancel- lorsville or Gettysburg—sporadic firing at first as the skirmish lines met and felt each other out, then halfhearted volleys while platoons came into the line, then the whole thing rising in intensity at last to a sus- tained drumroll of musketry. All that was lacking were the cannons— though some of those 10-gauge magnums banged nearly as loud.

The battlefield metaphor applied as well to the most effective hunt- ing technique employed in those days of abundance: The Drive. We hunted big fields, five or ten acres each of standing corn, maybe more. A couple of dozen men and boys would take part in these drives—half as "pushers" or drivers, the other half as "blockers," who got most of the shooting. The drives usually took place in midmorning or late after- noon, when the pheasants were busy feeding. Dogs were rarely used in these drives, though I recall that exceptions were made for a few well- trained Labradors and springers who could be trusted to stay coolly at heel until the shooting stopped. A whining or barking dog could ruin a drive early on by causing the alerted pheasants to leak out around the edges of the drive line before flushing. Any pheasant, wild born or pen raised, would rather run than fly—or so all the old-timers said.

While the blockers quietly took their positions at the bottom of the field, the pushers mustered at the far end, forming a shallow, cup- shaped line of men stationed no more than ten yards apart. Any wider a dispersal would allow birds to sneak back between the pushers. You wouldn't think so gaudy a creature as the ringneck—a bird, moreover, that weighs three pounds and measures three feet from beak to tail tip—could get so invisible so quickly. But it could. At a signal from the drive-master's police whistle, the pushers started forward. They had to march at a slow, steady, almost military pace—no straggling or sprinting ahead permitted—to keep the line intact and properly dressed. They zigzagged slightly as they marched, covering as much ground as possible. Because pushing was less likely than blocking to produce lots of good, fast shooting, most of the pushers were boys or young men. The rich old guys with their beer bellies got to block. Jack and I did a lot of pushing that week.

Gun safety was always on everyone's mind. The local newspapers and radio stations wouldn't let you forget it: TEEN KILLED ON FATAL PHEASANT DRIVE, FARGO RESIDENT BLINDED BY SHOTGUN BLAST. Here you had two rows of armed men, one approaching the other at a slow walk. Nerves on both sides were screwed to the yelping point, as if in impending battle. When the birds started to panic, to run and then to fly, the temptation would be strong—almost overpowering—to shoot straight ahead, and to shoot far too low. No one wanted to collect a faceful of No. 5s at close range. Nor to be the one who delivered it. The rules were clear and firmly enforced: Shoot only at high birds, no hens, and preferably only after they'd passed you, going away.

Here's what I recall of a typical drive near Slodeth, South Dakota, nearly half a century ago. A crisp, clear October morning, temperature in the low 50s, sky the blue of Betty Grable's peepers. The hollow banging of gunfire drums in the distance, all around us. Hendry Gobel, who owns the farmland we're hunting, stands in the middle of the drive line. He's a tall, fat, ruddy-cheeked farmboy-cum-entrepreneur in his early thirties, a decorated infantry veteran of World War II in Europe, now a big wheel in the Chamber of Commerce who doubles as the town's Chevy dealer and owns the local feed store as well. Wearing a flap-eared Elmer Fudd hunting cap and a red-and-black–checked deer hunting coat over his Oshkosh-B'gosh bib overalls, knee-high lace-up leather boots caked with Dakota mud and cow dung, he totes a scarred but well-oiled Winchester Model 12, its 30-inch barrel extended with a bulbous Polychoke. Hendry Gobel talks with a dutchy lilt. "Okey-dokey, poys, dere's lotza dem longtails in dis field today—see 'em in dere, down between da rows? When I plo da vissel, you guys *marsch!*"

"Jawohl, Herr Obersturmbahnführer," Jack mutters beside me. Yes, Hendry Gobel is a wee bit bossy.

But Hendry was right: We *could* see the pheasants down there between the rows, dozens at least, perhaps as many as a hundred of them, stalking jerkily, chickenlike, pecking at windfallen corncobs, the long-spurred cocks strutting in their gorgeous vanity while the drab hens scuttled humbly around their lords and masters. Nervously I shifted my gun, a well-worn old 12-gauge Winchester Model 97 pump that Jack's dad had loaned me for this hunt. It was his old gun. He was now shooting a Belgian Browning. My own single-shot 28-gauge wasn't quite the ticket for these birds and I'd left it back home in Wisconsin. Most of the guys I knew shot long-barreled, unplugged autoloaders or pumps on pheasants in those days. You rarely saw a double gun in the fields where the longtails played. My loaner was choked modified, but most of the others wore Polychokes. The bulges on the ends of the barrels made them look like tank cannons. Blockers set their Polychokes at open cylinder—very effective at close range—while pushers preferred modified or even improved cylinder settings for the longer shots they were likely to get. Some of the better or at least more confident shots even set them at full.

A sharp blast from Hendry Gobel's whistle set us in motion. I could see a few pheasants look up at the harsh sound—the cocks with their feathery blue "ears" atip—and begin scuttling toward the end of the field. We walked steadily, our weapons at port arms, gun butts thwacking the dry cornstalks, Hendry muttering occasional orders to slow down or speed up, or to keep our intervals neat and tidy. I could see sunlight glinting off the gun barrels of the blockers. About halfway down the field a rooster panicked and flew off, left to right. Hendry Gobel upped on the bird and dropped it as it cleared the right side of the field—a fifty-yard shot, maybe sixty. He was one of the more confident shooters.

At Hendry's shot other birds got up and some flew toward the blocking line. The shooting began, ragged at first, then faster.

"Schnell!" Hendry yelled. "Move faster, poys! Ve gotta get 'em up right now!"

We dog-trotted down the cornrows, our blood up, whooping and yelling like the Iron Brigade at Antietam, slapping the dry corn with our free hands, and the birds flushed almost in unison. The gunfire sounded like nonstop thunder, and suddenly it was raining pheasants. A cock came cackling right toward me, the ripped-metal blare getting louder with each beat of his wings. I skidded to a halt and swung with him as he swept past me, seeing his bright black eye locked on mine, then took him going away in a flurry of tiny rump feathers. Another came blowing past me and I swung and hit the trigger. Nothing. I'd forgotten to work the slide. By the time I shucked in another shell, most of the birds were dead or gone. All across the bottom of the field, feathers filtered down through the still morning air. But then as we walked the remaining distance toward the blockers, a single skulking rooster flushed from beneath my feet—straight up. I nailed him at the top of his rise just an instant before Jack shot. When that once-beauteous bird hit the ground it was nothing but rags.

"I guess it's yours," Jack said.

"What's left of him," I said. "Thanks for nothing."

I think we bagged more than fifty cock pheasants on that drive alone—the number that sticks in my fading memory is fifty-six. Of course I'd killed only two of them, and Jack had three plus his spoiling shot on my last bird. Hendry Gobel dropped five, one for each round in his gun, as did some of the other more experienced shooters, Jack's dad among them. It was slaughter, no doubt about it, but what the hell, why not? The birds were there in abundance—no, in overabundance. In a way they were a cash crop. The more of them we killed, the less corn they'd eat from Hendry Gobel's fields, and thus the more money he'd realize from his harvest. Not only that, but Hendry charged the guests who stayed in his big, roomy farmhouse fifteen dollars a day for the privilege, which included delicious meals heavy on roast pheasant stuffed with apples and sauerkraut.

But the drives, though exciting and highly productive, weren't near as much fun as the hunts Jack and I made alone during the early afternoons. While the old guys swilled schnapps and beer, played sheepshead, or took their sonorous siestas, Jack and I worked the edges of Gobel's swampland down near Tomahawk Slough for nooning roosters. Hendry's young black Lab, Mädchen, was only too glad to accompany us. In hip-boots and high spirits we slogged the marshes with Maddy porpoising ahead. It was fast, awkward shooting when she flushed a bird, with us standing ankle-deep in the muck, unable to shift our feet quickly, snap-shooting usually at big, fast-jumping cockbirds glimpsed only briefly through cattails and sawgrass against the hard blue sky. Sometimes we fell, knocked backward from the greasy-grass hummocks by the recoil of off-balance shots, but the water always felt good in that heat. I once emerged from a dunking with a mud turtle in my boot. We usually dragged back to the farmhouse before three o'clock, sweaty, flushed, reeking of foul-smelling swamp slime—but carrying at least half a dozen roosters between us. Gobel would *tut-tut* at our filth, grin fondly at our birds, sluice off the worst of the muck with a garden hose, and then it was off for another field drive. . . .

So that was my moment in Pheasant Heaven. I never thought I'd see its like again. But I was wrong, though it took a while.

Soon after the South Dakota excursion, I discovered girls. Then it was college, followed by a stint in the navy, marriage, fatherhood, a newspaper job in Milwaukee, then a move to New York and later Los Angeles for *Time* magazine. Then back to New York again for the Psychedelic Sixties—the Vietnam War, counterculture, assassinations, riots in the black ghettos, and suchlike follies.

Not much time for hunting with all of that going on. But I finally got back to it on a serious basis in 1964, when my wife and I bought a house in northernmost Westchester County, about an hour by commuter train from New York City. Behind the house lay nine hundred unposted acres of hilly, undeveloped woodland and overgrown hayfields. It was prime cover for grouse and woodcock back then—alder brakes down low for the bogsuckers, lots of ancient but still-fruitful apple trees, plenty of white pines for grouse to roost in, wild cherries, fox-grape hells, hickories, and big stands of sumac and doghair aspen up high, the whole of it crosshatched with miles of neatly built stone walls along which the partridge liked to skulk. But there were always a few pheasants hanging out in the uncut meadows that dotted the second-growth woods. I soon had a canine team to help me harass them—a big yellow Lab named Simba and a keen but slightly wacky German shorthair called Max.

These pheasants were the wild descendants of stock initially released before World War II, not pen-raised birds. They were fast afoot, veritable Roger Bannisters of roosterdom, and extremely reluctant to fly even when pinned dead to rights by the pointer. But Simba quickly learned that whenever Max locked up, his best bet was to circle out beyond the bird, then move back in on it. We got our share of flushes. I still remember one longtail that almost eluded us. It was a snowy day in November. We'd hunted the long wooded ridge at the top of a big meadow, then struck off down the brush-grown stone wall that bisected the field. From the way the dogs acted I knew there was a pheasant running ahead of them. Simba finally got in front of it near the bottom and the bird flushed—a rooster. But before I could mount the gun, the bird had lighted in the uppermost branches of a tall ash tree, from which lofty vantage point he looked down and gave us the raspberry in the form of a jeering, cocksure cackle.

What to do? I'd gotten religion by then and refused on principle to pot the bird out of the tree. We waited it out—five minutes, ten minutes—hoping he'd get nervous and fly. He didn't. Finally I leaned my gun within easy reach against the ash trunk, made a snowball, and threw it at the pheasant. I zinged half a dozen snowballs at that cockbird before I threw a strike. He whirled and launched; I grabbed the gun, fumbled at the safety—and missed him twice. He soared back up the way we'd come down, finally landing at the top of the field a quarter of a mile away.

The dogs seemed amused at my bad marksmanship. "All right, lads," I told them gruffly, "let's start hiking." We plodded back uphill through the ankle-deep snow, halting near where I'd marked the rooster down. Up there, thanks to the wind, the snow lay thinner on the ground. The field had been mowed in the late summer and the grass was short, just the tips of it showing through the fluffy white cover. Any gaudy cockbird hunkered down in that stubble would have stood out like a zit on a teenager's face. No bird in sight. But then I noticed a straight line of taller grass, about a foot high, that grew along a fallen strand of wire, the remnants of an electric fence long out of use. I started walking the wire with the dogs just ahead of me. About halfway along, the snow suddenly erupted as the rooster took flight— from a patch of grass you wouldn't think could hide a field mouse. I rolled him twenty yards out. . . .

That's the way it was with those pheasants of the Near Northeast. I pretty much despaired of ever again seeing the kind of nonstop, slam-bang pheasant shooting I'd enjoyed in the heartland as a boy. Meanwhile, burned out on global violence, I'd quit *Time* and joined up with *Sports Illustrated,* where I covered the gentler worlds of pro football, motor sports, and the outdoors. One of my beats was the Formula I racing circuit, and in 1973 at the U.S. Grand Prix in Watkins Glen, New York, I met Lord Alexander Hesketh. Then twenty-three years old, he was a plump, witty, wealthy, and somewhat flaky Brit who had entered a new F-I team into the lists. His driver then was the late James Hunt, a handsome, nervy young stalwart who went on to win the World Driving Championship but achieved greater name recognition when the actor Richard Burton stole his wife. Over dinner one night in Corning, New York, Alexander was telling me about his baronial estate, Easton Neston, north of London. "We've got loads of pheasants," His Lordship said. "Why don't you pop over some time for a shoot?"

I pounced on the invitation like a springer on a covey of quail.

In January of 1974, the last month of the English pheasant season, I flew to London and then headed north, roughly a two-hour drive from Piccadilly Circus. Easton Neston occupies seven thousand acres near the town of Towcester (rhymes with "boaster"). The Hesketh manor house, built largely of marble, was begun in the late 1680s and completed half a century later. The ceilings in some of its rooms were thirty feet high. You could park a Rolls Royce in any of the downstairs fireplaces. Entering the house, I was first impressed by the sepulchral chill, then by the sight of a full-mounted brown bear rearing up in a dark hallway corner. Wintry light glinted off suits of armor arrayed behind the bear. On the table in the entry hall lay a paperback copy of

M.A.S.H. Goes to Maine, a huge bowie knife, and a guest book full of the scrawled signatures of Churchills, Windsors, and Douglas-Homes. In the echoing dining room, a brace of Rubens paintings added a touch of warmth to the background behind the butler's eyes. The erect figure of a stuffed snowy owl glowered from one corner. I stood near the crackling fireplace, warming my bum as I sipped a welcoming glass of sherry, and admired the tapestries on the walls. Beyond the mullions of the rain-streaked casement windows I could see pheasants strutting haughtily on the putting-green lawns. I was a long way from Hendry Gobel's farmhouse in South Dakota.

At dinner that evening the rest of the guests assembled, and after a few minutes it became evident that what we Americans take for satirical novels of English country life are nothing more than straight reportage. Consider if you will the Lambton sisters, Anne and Rose. Anne was small and pale with the sharp-toothed grin of a dolphin. She affected a freaky air and a faux-Cockney accent—"wiv" for "with," for example—and feigned a total incomprehension of affairs in the "real world."

"Are vey still hafing vose 'orrible bombs in Londing?" she asked. "Oy 'aven't bean vare in mumfs. Oh pigs! Oy spilt me caviar!" She laughed with an oinking snort.

Her sister, Rose, was taller but even more out of touch, a whiter shade of pale with dyed, dark-red hair. She'd brought her pet dog along, a tetchy little shelty bitch that lurked beneath the dining table nipping at ankles and whining now and then like a household ghost. Next to Rose sat Andrew Fraser, a younger son of Lord Lovat who led the No. 4 Commandos during World War II. A keen shot, dark, trim, and amused, Andrew seemed very fit—except for his right eye, which he'd damaged quite severely not long before when he threw a firecracker into a bonfire. "The surgeons removed the lens," he explained, very cool and dispassionate, "but the rest of the eye is still sound. They say that perhaps I can wear a contact lens and regain part of the sight, but until then I'm afraid my shooting is a bit off form."

Across from Fraser sat Robert Fermor-Hesketh, Alexander's younger brother. (A third brother, John, the youngest, was not present.

An even keener shot than Fraser, John usually spent the bird season, from the Glorious Twelfth of August to the end of January, traveling around Britain in a car, complete with a built-in bed, shooting partridge, pheasants, grouse, woodcock, and wildfowl wherever he could glean an invitation.) Robert Hesketh, or "Bobs" as he was known, proved a shorter, trimmer version of Alexander, who in those days at least stood six-four and weighed in at 240 pounds. Wide-shouldered and flat-bellied by contrast, Bobs sported a leonine mane and beard. Tough, bouncy, and glowering, he too was a crack shot and competitor, as would be evidenced the next morning under the flighted pheasants of Easton Neston.

Dawn broke through a fine, cold rain—little more than a mist at first, but with teeth in it. I'd debated long and hard over dressing for the shoot in English style—Wellies, moleskin breeks, Norfolk jacket, ascot, Barbour coat, oiled cotton shooting cap, maybe even one of those classy fold-down shooting sticks. But no, I couldn't go that route—too phony, too foppish. Instead I dressed in my usual upland attire: scuffed but well-greased Russell boots; khaki canvas brush pants and game jacket, worn over a red-checked wool shirt, and topped off with a scruffy Jones cap replete with the requisite grouse tailfeather. Let them sneer their Limey sneers at the country-bred cousin from over the pond. I was a descendant of Natty Bumppo, by Gawd, and I'd shoot their eyes out. . . .

Like hell I would.

We were eight guns that day, each man backed up by a loader to keep his matched pair of doubles primed and ready. My guns were slim, elegant, side-locked Bosses, long-barreled 12-bores, of course, courtesy of His Lordship (though only for the day, alas). My loader was a short, cheery assistant gamekeeper named Sid Atker, who chattered merrily as we slogged though a field of winter wheat to the first stand of the day.

"Ah, yes," quoth Sid, "most of the land is under cultivation, but His Lordship maintains about seven thousand pheasant on the estate, that he does, and shoots it only six or eight times a season, killing up to eight hundred birds a go. But today I reckon we won't kill no more than five or six hundred, not with the weather like this—watch your step there, sir, it's mucky goin', innit?—no, this rain will keep 'em from flyin', too heavy they get in the wet like this, they'd rather run than fly,"—and where had I heard that before?—"but here come the beaters now, sir; you'd better get ready."

The beaters, some fifty men and boys and a few small girls from the neighboring village, pushed through the first patch of wood, trilling and chirruping and bellowing to frighten the pheasants ahead of them, thwacking the bushes and tree trunks with their clubs, now and then coshing a hare or rabbit as it tried to cut back through the line. The gamekeeper, a red-faced sergeant-major type who ran the shoot with an iron hand, directed the beaters with his police whistle (just like Hendry Gobel).

As the beaters neared the wood edge we could see the pheasants milling—tall, tan, scuttling figures, reluctant to approach the open ground. Then they exploded with a rattle of wet wings and lined out toward the guns where we stood a hundred yards away in the open field, each man fifty yards from his nearest neighbor. By the time the birds reached us, they were at full flight speed and thirty yards high.

Guns began slamming all up and down the line. Blue smoke hung suspended in the drizzle and drifted slowly in the light, cold air. The birds, when hit, seemed to double in size, their feathers puffing, then crumpled and fell with wings all askew. They thumped hard on the wet ground. Then again that strange phenomenon, only witnessed when clouds of birds are killed directly overhead. What appeared to be bronze snowflakes began to fall from the sky: pheasant feathers. Soon they were thick as a blizzard. I caught a glimpse, between shots, of James Hunt poking awkwardly at a high double and missing both birds. He had never shot before.

I saw Andrew Fraser, bad eye and all, center a cockbird, then with his left barrel knock feathers from another that sloped away to fall behind the shooting line. Not to worry, the dogs—thick-bodied, keen-eyed Labs that waited phlegmatically to the rear—would gather it up later with the other wounded birds. I watched Robert Hesketh just long enough to see him drop five doubles in a row, faster than it takes to write this sentence, all of the birds falling within ten yards of where he stood. None of them thrashed for even a moment. As for me, on that first drive, I killed some birds, but wounded or missed a lot more.

While the dogs collected the dead and the cripples, we guns moved to the next drive, a gloomy spot known as The Wilderness. My post was at the edge of the wood, in a cut among some pines. The birds came out of the trees fast and low, appearing in full flight only ten yards ahead of me as they bored through the feathery upper branches. It was snapshooting of the sort familiar to North American grouse and woodcock shooters, and my score quickly improved. I knocked down a clean double, then another, then a string of singles, mixed in with a few fretful misses, then a final double. Already my shoulder was aching. The Bosses, beautiful as they looked, were clearly too short for my length of pull.

Then a figure emerged from the stiffening rain. It was Alexander's mother, Kisty, the widow lady of the manor, a strong, handsome, friendly woman with a liking for America and Americans. Except for bright red knee socks, she was clad all in black—black breeks, black jacket, a wide-brimmed Andalusian-style hat, and a black eyepatch. She'd lost the sight of one eye as the result of a recent car crash, but the eyepatch gave her a jolly piratical look. Her good eye twinkled through the mist.

"I've been watching you, Yank," she said. "You shot well in this close covert. How do you like it so far?"

"Glorious carnage," I said.

She laughed. "Strange people, the English," she mused, knocking gobbets of clay from her boots with a gnarled walking stick. The mud fell with a sodden thump on a dead cock pheasant that lay at her feet. "They call this recreation."

The rest of the day was a blur of falling birds, my ears ringing with the hollow, ragged rage of 12-bore explosions, the hallooing of the beaters, the strident chirp of the gamekeeper's whistle. The whole world— black, gray, brown, green—smelled of blood and burnt gunpowder. At one point, a pure white pheasant flushed and swiveled its way through the barrage, miraculously escaping unhit. At another, a small, shaggy animal that resembled a long-legged pig emerged from the woods, did a double take on seeing the guns, and bounded back to safety. "Chinese barking deer," explained Kisty, who was strolling past at the moment. "A few of them wandered in here from an estate farther south. Ugly little things, though, aren't they? We don't shoot 'em."

The final tally for the day was 580 pheasant, sixteen duck (mallards that flushed from ponds in the fields), a dozen woodcock, and eight wood pigeons. Only a middling score for Easton Neston. "I'd hoped for at least twelve hundred," Hesketh told me later. This was not simply a matter of bruised pride: English landowners sell the game killed in such shoots to restaurants in London and elsewhere, using the money thus earned to defray the costs of gamekeepers, beaters, loaders, and so on. A poor shoot is money out of pocket. The gamekeepers laid the birds out for us near the manor house, on the putting-green lawn. It was quite a sight. I asked Sid Atker if he'd kept count on how many I'd shot.

"You did right well for a newcomer, sir," he said. "I counted seventy-eight pheasant that fell to your gun, plus a couple of woodcock and a pigeon or two. Right well indeed, I'd say."

Later, back in my room for a welcome, blood-warming bath, I noticed that my shooting arm was black and blue from shoulder to elbow, the inevitable legacy of ill-fitting guns. But it was a small price to pay for the experience. Once again the heavens had blessed me with the manna of falling feathers. No, we hadn't done as well as the shooting party at Lord Stamford's park, which over four days in early January of 1864 had tallied 4,045 pheasant, 3,902 rabbits, 860 hares, and fifty-nine woodcock. Nor would I personally pose much of a threat to the shooting record of the late Lord Ripon, who between 1867 and 1904 settled the hash of 142,343 pheasant, 97,759 partridge, 56,460 grouse, 29,858 rabbits, and 27,686 hares. Frankly, I doubt that anyone will. Yet I'm glad that I had at least two chances in my lifetime—in the South Dakota of 1948 and the English countryside of 1974—to see and shoot at masses of flighted pheasants, wild clouds of them.

It was glorious carnage indeed.

CONNOISSEURS OF COVER

he essence
of American
upland bird
hunting is a
long hard walk
through tough
cover. That's
why they call
it rough shoot-
ing. I've taken nonhunting friends along on some
of my more leisurely strolls after grouse and woodcock, and to a man or woman they've emerged
exhausted from the woods at the end of those
hikes—leg-weary, drenched in sweat, bleeding from
multiple thorn slashes, and totally baffled as to
where they've been. "Hey, look!" one woman said
as we emerged from the woods at the end of an
afternoon's outing. "There's a truck just like yours,
parked right over there in that thicket!" When I
told her we'd made a big circle through the woods

she just couldn't believe it. "I thought we'd gone in a straight line," she said. "Well, with maybe a little bit of up and down in it?"

In England and on the Continent, they hunt birds in a much more civilized manner. Shooters draw for position at the beginning of a drive, then stand about waiting in the open fields while beaters hired from the local village push the game birds—pheasants or grouse or partridge—to the edge of the dense cover in which they hide, where-upon the birds are forced to fly, right over the guns. By the time they reach the firing line the birds are at speed, flying high and fast, and it is true that they present difficult targets. But the shooter is aided and abetted by a loader, usually a wiry little Andy Capp clone with a face like a Jack Russell terrier's and the moves to match, who grabs away each Boss or Purdey's or H&H double as rapidly as it's emptied and slaps a reloaded second gun into the shooter's hands, then reloads the empty one, twisting, bobbing and whirling like a dervish, *bang-bang, bang-bang, bang-bang* . . . like that, all day long. On a good day, bags of a thousand birds are not unusual.

But that kind of shooting is not for most rough-and-ready American hunters. We pride ourselves on our pioneer/frontiersman/bushwhacker heritage. Historically most of our shooting has been not on the estates of the wealthy (except for the odd poaching foray, perhaps), where the game is raised by keepers and only swells need apply, but rather on wild land at the edges of towns, often public land. You get touches of the old English gentlemanly tradition in, say, a dove shoot, where the gunner sits comfortably in a blind amid cutover corn or soybeans and the birds fly to him at his leisure, or on a traditional southern quail hunt replete with saddle horses and mule-drawn wagons for the dogs. But real upland hunting, American style, means pounding the hills and swamps and thickets, usually behind a dog who is also a friend, and suffering the slings and arrows of outrageous cover in a kind of prepaid atonement for the bird lives we hope to extinguish. Thus over the years, like it or not, we become connoisseurs of cover in all its hellish guises.

We learn early on the treachery of alders. The footing is inevitably miserable in an alder brake, the wet, mucky ground littered with the rotting corpses of expired or moribund earlier growth just waiting to trip you up. You step on the leaning trunk of a seemingly sound alder to hoist yourself over and it breaks just as a woodcock flushes, depositing you and your gun facedown down in the muck—an intimate introduction to the reality of the mud bat's world. The upper stories of an alder thicket are an ideal aerobatic playground for flighted woodcock. Provided you can poke your gun up through the branches and achieve a bit of a swing. Let's say you've just centered a vaulting woodcock and are in the act of hitting the trigger—when the bird suddenly reverses direction and simultaneously soars straight up like a helicopter. . . . Another miss. Hunting alder brakes, you soon develop a woodcocklike ability of your own to twist, sidestep, duck, bow, lean, lurch, and waddle your way through the infernal stuff, at the same time keeping your gun at high port arms and ready for an instant shot wherever it offers, or else you just don't hunt them anymore. If you're sure you hit a flushing woodcock but neither you nor your dog can find it, always check the upper branches of the alders. A number of times I've despaired of finding dead woodcock on the ground only to look up at last and find them sprawled on a bed of interlaced twigs at eye level or higher.

Fox grapes often provide excellent feeding cover for grouse. In years when they're producing abundantly, I've sometimes flushed as many as a dozen ruffs from a grape patch no bigger than my living room. But grouse have a propensity for flushing just when you're hung up in a tangle of grapevines, or stooped over trying with your free hand to break the stranglehold that a vine with a Hulk Hogan grip has just thrown around your throat. I often sidestep to open up a better shot when a grouse flushes, but I quickly learned not to do so in grapevines after I fell on my keister a few times just as I was about to shoot—tripped up by the wily vines of *Vitis labrusca*.

Wild apple and oak groves also offer their hazards, especially in years of bumper crops. I've seen sure-footed dogs, in canine four-wheel drive, go charging into an oak thicket and suddenly lose it, skidding sideways as they hit the carpet of acorns covering the ground. Little green apples are just as bad, for dog and man alike. Normally during bird season I wear a pair of old, well-worn Russell boots with cleated, hard-compound soles, but during years of bumper apple or acorn crops when I know I'm going to be hunting a lot of these treacherous coverts, I pull on a pair of L. L. Bean boot-pacs with leather uppers and rubber bottoms. The soft rubber soles with their chainlike grip seem to give better traction on such surfaces.

Thornapple coverts can be a pain, quite literally. Not only are the long, sharp spikes capable of penetrating a dog's pads as well as the heavy canvas fabric of brush pants, hunting shirts, and shooting vests, but they can pierce boot leather, too. Shooting glasses are a good idea in all kinds of grouse cover, but especially in thornapples. A limber twig laden with two-inch stilettos can all too easily whip back and skewer an unprotected eyeball. Even a slap on the eye by an unspiked branch can hurt like the devil—the ache is akin to that of a kick in the goolies.

Blackberry brambles and clumps of multiflora rosebushes abound in my corner of grouse country. Inevitably, even if I carry the shotgun above my head, one snaky, serrated blackberry stalk will somehow manage to rip that hand, usually leaving a trail of slow-welling blood that becomes evident only later when I raise the hand to wipe the sweat from my forehead. I've taken to wearing a light leather shooting glove on my nontrigger hand, the hand I use to push brambles aside as I press my way through them; and for a while I even tried a glove on my shoot-ing hand. But the glove diminished the sensitivity I seem to need if I'm to shoot consistently on flushing birds, and I'd rather suffer a few more brier slashes than miss a few more birds. A glove on the trigger finger is like wearing a condom, safer perhaps but not quite as much fun.

The lesser hazards of my bird coverts include the wiry, waist-high brush known as "steepletop," an extremely tough medium to wade through; the man-high thickets of doghair aspen in which grouse are prone to lurk, and which have a playful propensity for slapping you in the crotch as you transit them; the delightfully named "honeysuckle" jungles that look so fragile yet are impossible to bull through without getting tripped up; the low, dark snares of ground junipers that delight in seeing an armed man sprawl on his butt; the dense groves of young spruce in which grouse sometimes are to be found, but which often make the swinging, or even the raising, of a gun impossible. Spruces are only too happy to poke you in the eye, occasionally reaching in behind your shooting glasses to do so. Even the earth itself holds surprises. One mountainous slope behind my house is full of cleverly camouflaged seep springs, into which I'm likely to step crotch-deep when least expecting it. Not only do I get a boot full of ice water for my troubles, but a grouse always flies precisely at the moment of my lopsided lurch. Ah yes—they know, they know!

Then there are the laurel jungles of the Appalachians, the catbriers of the Deep South, the Spanish bayonets of Texas, the sagebrush and prickly pear wastelands of the West, the wait-a-bit thorns of Africa. . . . I could go on and on, if only my legs weren't so weary and my hide so lamentably lacerated.

Still, that's why we call it hunting, not shopping. What I mean is, it's not like walking up to the poultry counter in the IGA or Dean & Deluca to select the best-looking bird that will fit your budget. Oh sure, you can suffer the anguish of the damned while shopping, but at least they don't grow thorns in the aisles yet. Even so, I'd rather go hunting for my meat.

PARTNERS

In bird hunting, as in real life, there are loners and there are party animals. Waterfowl shooting, like the European-style driven shoots, is almost always a group effort: A gaggle of gunners crouches dankly in a duck blind, one of them working the call and signaling the shot when the birds finally toll to the decoys. A dove shoot is similar, though there's no need for a caller.

Upland hunting, on the other hand, lends itself more happily to the solo effort: the lone turkey hunter hunkered in the woods at dawn, listening closely and occasionally emitting a raspy, plaintive yelp, or a man and his dog just cruising the coverts to see what they can see. Antisocial, perhaps, but in this era of too many people that's probably no bad thing.

Still, though I'm a loner by nature, there are times when I enjoy pounding the partridge coverts and woodcock brakes with a companion or two. It all depends on my partners. Hunting with longtime friends, especially men you only see from bird season to bird season, can be pleasant—catching up on domestic or career developments, hearing new jokes, recalling hunts from the past whether they were successful or calamitous—all of this can give a day in the upland coverts the fine, warm aura of a family reunion. But only if the companion is a sensible shooter. Each man hunts at his own pace, and a good partner will adjust his to that of his host, just as the host should defer the easy shots, or at least the first few of them, to his guest. I certainly won't hunt more than once with a man who waves his gun muzzles all over the sky, or points a gun at me however inadvertently, or takes wild shots without knowing for certain what he's firing at. I won't hunt with a man who mistreats a gundog, either verbally or physically, however grievous the dog's errors. I won't hunt with a game hog, nor with a man who shows contempt for what he's shooting. Competition has no place in the hunting field. It turns birds and animals into mere prizes in a tawdry game of one-on-one, markers on the ugly map of an ego trip, no better than the frozen gobblers offered for the best score at a turkey shoot. Save the testosterone for the skeet range or the tennis court.

I learned these lessons in companionable comportment the hard way, during a dozen or so trips afield over four or five seasons with a fellow I'll call Lee Harvey Woolworth. I still can't figure out why I ever agreed to hunt with him. Maybe I was desperate for companionship.

Lee was a carpenter in Westchester County when my wife and I moved there in the early 1960s, and we met through the local nursery school, where both of our sons were incarcerated for a part of each weekday. In the course of our conversations, while waiting for the boys to be sprung, it developed that Lee was a bird hunter. New to the area, I was only too eager to get out in the field with him, in hopes at least of learning the location of his coverts. But you get what you pay for.

As it turned out, we most often hunted the vast chain of fields and thickets on the nine hundred acres behind my house. Lee showed me only three small coverts of his own, none of them worth diddly.

He was a tall, lanky, dark-haired guy in his early thirties who talked with a perpetual sneer on his lips. Though he came from a wealthy, well-educated family, he seemed to take pride in bad grammar, laughing at my use of proper English and downright guffawing whenever I waxed literary. "You know what your trouble is?" he'd say. "You hang out too much with them *suède-o-intellectuals*." I soon learned to stop pointing out beautiful scenery to him, or—God forbid—quoting from the nature poets. No "season of mists and mellow fruitfulness" for Lee. He was a meat hunter, plain and simple. To him the ruffed grouse was a "pa'tridge," and he furrowed his brow in mock incomprehension whenever I called the bird by its rightful name. "Grouches" was his best translation of the word, as in "I seen a flock a' them grouches in the apple trees behind your place yestiddy, let's go blast us a bunch."

He hated hawks, owls, and what he called "tweety birds," and when he missed a shot on game, he often took out his frustration on the next blackbird, grackle, starling, or chickadee that flew by, and once on a kestrel hovering high over a field we were crossing.

"Why in the hell did you shoot it?" I asked, enraged.

"They're pests," he said. "They kill pa'tridges and pheasants."

I picked up the hawk by a shattered wing. It was no larger than a mourning dove.

"Bullshit," I explained. "They hunt mice and songbirds. That's why they call them sparrow hawks."

"Aw, whadda *you* know about it?" And he stomped off toward the next covert.

Every hunt with Lee was a sprint. Though I'm tall, he was taller, with legs that seemed to reach to his Adam's apple, and he tried to walk me into the ground at every opportunity. He usually did. Entering a stretch of cover, one man to either side with my dog ostensibly working between us, Lee would disappear into the foliage and emerge at the far end with a furlong's lead. Thus he flushed most of the birds far out of my sight, and often his own sight as well. I'd hear grouse going off like bursts from a burp gun, rarely challenged by a blast from Lee's 12-gauge.

My dog, a polite young black Lab named Peter, of course would move at the faster man's pace, staying ten or fifteen yards ahead of him. Whenever I whistled him over to my side of the covert, Lee would quickly call him back to his. Since I usually hunt with flushing retrievers, which rely to some extent on foot scent to locate their prey, my natural pace in heavy cover is slow. Lee had my poor pup rushing through dense brush where he couldn't pick up even body scent, suppressed as it was by the leafy shrubbery, and I'm sure we bypassed many birds, especially tight-lying woodcock. But Lee had no use for woodcock anyway. "Bogsuckers" he called them. "How can you eat them things?" he'd ask when I killed and pocketed one. "They slurp worms."

"So do bass," I said, "and you eat *them*, don't you?"

"That's different," he'd say, and hurry off to another thicket.

Lee was a fair shot, and I'm sure would have been a better one if he used anything but the gun he preferred for all fieldwork. It was an old Winchester pump with a full-choked, 30-inch tube, its varnished stock scarred and scabby and most of the bluing worn off the barrel. He could mount it like lightning, though, and work it like the proverbial slide trombone. As with pounding coverts, it was a point of pride with Lee to beat me to the shot if he possibly could. I remember a hen pheasant we flushed one Sunday afternoon as we neared a brushy stone wall between two overgrown hayfields. It was a hot, close day and Peter didn't get birdy until he was almost on top of the luckless hen. I saw the dog light up and began to raise my gun—a light little 20-gauge Daly—but as the bird whirred and flew, I noticed the long, pointy tail and knew that it was a pheasant. In those days, thanks to some archaic New York blue law, pheasants could not be hunted on Sundays, though grouse and woodcock were legal. But Lee's cannon was at his shoulder in a flash, and the bird was lunchmeat before it was ten yards out. I saw it explode in a slurry of meat and brown fluff. He'd centered it, sure enough.

"Oops!" Lee said. "I thought it was one a' them grouches. But it was a pretty shot, wasn't it? I sure beat you to the draw that time!"

Though the bird was unsalvageable, he stuffed the pulped mess into his game pocket anyway, something more to brag on when he got home.

The only time I've ever been shot while bird hunting was thanks to Lee Woolworth. Again it took place along one of those old stone walls. This one led uphill from a boggy stand of alder and sumac, forming the upright column of a capital T where it abutted another overgrown wall at the top of the covert. It was late afternoon, the light fading, as I pushed up the right-hand side of the wall, invisible to Lee, who was working to my left. We were about ten yards apart. This time I had somehow gotten the lead in our customary footrace, and had just reached the upper, crosswise wall when Peter got birdy. I heard Lee call to the dog, down there about twenty yards behind me, and was climbing the wall when it flushed—directly on a line from Lee to me. I could see it blurring toward me.

"Hey, don't shoot. . . ." I yelled, to alert him to my presence.

Wham!

He cut loose anyway. Even as I felt the edge of Lee's pattern lace me from face to knees, I saw the bird tumble dead in the weeds.

"Well, you got him," I said. "And you got me, too."

Lee came stumbling up through the brush, broke clear, picked up his bird, and finally looked uphill in my direction.

"What, did you say I *hit* you?"

"Damn straight," I told him. My legs had started to sting, and with my fingertips I could now feel a few size 7 $1/2$ shot lying under the skin of my cheekbone, hard and lumpy as incipient boils.

"Aw, don't be a crybaby," Lee said with his customary sneer. "It happens to everyone. I been dusted lotsa times. Look at it this way, at least you ain't dead or blinded."

We picked the shot out of my face and legs with the point of a jackknife and called it a day.

Shortly thereafter, Lee and his family moved to Florida. I can't say I missed him as a hunting partner, though oddly enough he was capable of wit and charm in other venues, and our wives and children were good friends. But despite his many faults in the field, I'm grateful to him in a way. Now I know what to avoid when somebody new asks me to go hunting with him.

THE BOGSUCKER NIGHTMARE

I t was a nightmare in red and white—a season out of joint. In all my years of bird hunting I've never seen anything like it, nor do I hope to again.

On Sunday, October 4, 1987, barely a week into the new season and only three days after woodcock had opened, a paralyzing blizzard slammed into the Northeast without warning, blanketing east-central New York, southwestern Vermont where I live, and much of interior New England with up to twenty inches of wet, heavy snow. It toppled power-transmission towers, downed electrical and phone lines, overloaded the branches of trees still fully leafed in their gaudy fall colors and snapped them in sharp, irregular cracks that, at the storm's height, sounded like the Siege of Khe Sanh. Where a day or two before, piles of bright, tidily raked leaves had smoldered sweetly in the autumn air, now there was only shivering dismay. Some towns went without power for more than a week.

But really the storm was no big deal for most people. Preparedness is the watchword of life in small-town New England. In most rural homes the wood was already in, the Coleman lanterns and kerosene lamps fueled and mantled, fridges and freezers well stocked. It was kind of pleasant, being snowbound. We melted snow in pots on the tops of our wood stoves, cooked meals over wood fires or propane ranges, hauled buckets of water from nearby brooks to keep the toilets flushing, and read at night by lamplight. No television, of course, but I count that a blessing.

My only worry was for the game birds.

It would be tough going for the turkey flocks, but I've known those big, hardy birds to shovel their way through a couple of feet of new snow to get at beechnut crops beneath it, and this year there was plenty of beech mast. It's hard-crusted snow that starves those birds, and this storm, thank God, had not been followed by a deep freeze. Not yet. They'd make it.

The ruffed grouse, I knew, would weather the blizzard in good shape. Grouse actually thrive on deep snow, blasting deep into drifts in the dead of winter to bed down in their insulating warmth. Snow would protect the partridge from predation by foxes, coyotes, goshawks, and great horned owls, and since the grouse is an opportunistic feeder he'd emerge from his snowy den only briefly, to hop up into the popples and gobble aspen buds.

But what about woodcock—in some ways my favorite among eastern upland game birds? For the "bogsucker" it's earthworms or nothing. With snow lying deep on the ground, or a hard frost in it, a woodcock must tighten his belt—at least until he can fly on to softer, wormier, more southerly pastures. There'd been plenty of resident woodcock in my coverts that year. I'd heard at least six males peenting the previous spring, and seen them spiraling high in their sky dances as early as April.

Since each female typically lays four eggs (buff-colored, speckled, hidden carefully under shrubs or among dead leaves on the ground), there could with luck be as many as three dozen timberdoodles in my home coverts that fall. I'd been looking forward to a banner year on both grouse and woodcock, and already my black Lab Luke and I had bagged a few of each, but missed many more. (That was because of the dense, early-season leaf cover, I told myself, though Luke probably laid the blame where it rightly belonged: on shabby shooting.)

Then came the blizzard.

Had the woodcock sensed it coming and departed to more open country before it hit? Maybe, maybe not. By daylight I saw gangs of robins hopping forlornly along the road edges as the snow melted. Robins, like woodcock, are migrant worm hunters. They hadn't fled before the storm, nor had the phoebes or many of the fall warblers. I'd read somewhere that woodcock can put up with three days of hunger before they feel compelled to move on. They have plenty of grease in their guts and are covered with good, warm plumage. But one night I stepped outside for a moment and heard, high in the moonlit sky above me, a flock of Canada geese, invisible, yelping their way toward the south, well ahead of their normal schedule. Were the woodcock moving as well? Or would they tough it out?

In my dreams those first nights after the storm, I saw woodcock huddled beneath crooked, snow-shrouded alder limbs, their long bills tucked into their chest feathers, wet eyes shining in the gloom. Then I dreamed them toppling sideways, their eyes dimming as snow sifted down to cover them, their russet feathers ragged in the night wind, frost climbing their thin pink toes.

Three days after the storm I awoke before dawn. The moon shone cold and pitiless on a world of ice. I dreaded going into my woodcock coverts that day for fear of what Luke and I would find. It might be like walking onto a battlefield the morning after the guns went quiet.

Over the years I've found two distinct kinds of woodcock coverts around these parts. The most productive kind are the "flight coverts" used by birds moving down from their summer breeding grounds in Quebec, the Canadian Maritimes, and northern Vermont. When the flight birds are in, there's no mistaking it. They're present in great numbers—eight, ten, twenty, and on one memorable day fully sixty woodcock in a single ten-acre patch, according to my hunting journal. These flight coverts are usually close to water.

On the other hand, the coverts preferred by resident birds, which have had all summer to discover where water lies, can be anywhere in the upland hardwoods, in stands of doghair aspen, or on the edges of alder or willow brakes—almost any damp place you'd expect to find worms. Rarely will the dog flush more than two or three woodcock out of these resident coverts.

The resident woodcock are scattered, almost territorially, it seems to me, and you have to pound to find them. And pounding hilly country is the essence of upland game.

It was my first day out after the storm, a Wednesday, and I decided to hunt only the resident coverts. Luke would sniff out any storm-killed birds in short order. Though he wouldn't pick up a bird not fresh-killed by the gun, I'd be able to tell from his bearing that he was onto something dead, and spot it lying somewhere under his nose.

But if we moved no birds at all from the resident covers, I could safely (if sadly) assume that the woodcock had gotten out before the storm—perhaps on the three-quarter moon of the previous Friday night. Whether they'd made it clear of the snow zone, of course, I would never know for sure. Or at least not until the next spring, when I'd be able to see and hear how many had returned to mate.

There was always the slim chance that I'd find the same birds in the resident coverts that had been there before the storm, alive and well, or at least sitting up and taking nourishment. But I forced myself to keep that hope well hidden under the dry leaves of logic. I really expected to find the aftermath of disaster.

When we entered the woods on that windy afternoon, they did indeed resemble a battlefield. Everywhere the limbs of young popples, gaunt birches, and old apple trees hung shattered from the weight of the snow. Raw wood gleamed bright in the intermittent sunlight, and green leaves lay dying under skifts of settled, dirty snow. Ferns, leaves, and weeds lay matted, as if they'd been trampled flat by the feet of a mile-high giant. The damp air had a sour smell to it when the sun disappeared behind racing clouds. I shied from imagined corpses.

The first of our woodcock coverts drew blank, except for a solitary grouse that got up wild about forty yards out. Then another grouse blew about a hundred yards farther on. So the partridge had made it, as I knew they would.

As we entered the second covert—a stand of young aspens on a sidehill studded with feathery white pines—Luke got birdy. His tail wagged faster, his ears cocked upward, the ruff along his neck and back rose, and he glowed even blacker than normal. His pace slowed and he nosed forward, inch by inch, shuddering with self-imposed restraint. Then the birds got up right in front of his jaws—two woodcock together, a straightaway twisting double, but I didn't even raise the shotgun. For all I knew, just yet, they were the sole survivors of the storm.

The next covert produced a single woodcock, a big, plump female by the look of her. She caught us both by surprise, and I tangled my feet spinning to swing on her. She blasted strongly across an open field and pitched into a dense alder patch across a roaring black brook. I marked the spot well. We could always jump her again if we chose.

We entered the fourth and final covert of the afternoon with high hopes and blood in our eyes. So far it had been a typical woodcock swing, the same pattern of flushes we'd encountered before the storm. Luke had poked dutifully into a flight covert along our route and frisked it well, producing nothing. The flight birds weren't down yet, and that was a relief.

The last time we'd hit this resident covert, two days before the blizzard, it had held four woodcock, one of which we'd killed. If all was right with the world, there should still be three in there.

We went in.

It was a long, low alder thicket, rising uphill from a brook to fan out at the top into young hardwoods still bright with color. Down near the brook, Luke jumped a 'cock just where we knew one should be, but it got a tree between us and I didn't shoot.

A short way uphill, Luke flushed another. Which I missed with both barrels. Luke glared back at me with his customary censure. I'd gotten used to that look, over the years, but it always stung. Okay, Boss, I promised him, I'll try harder next time. . . .

Up near the top, out of the alders now and into the hardwoods, the third woodcock rose from the threat of Luke's hustle. It blew out toward the open, twisting like a scatback, and I shot with full confidence. Like the closing of a prayer book, the bird folded and thumped down dead among the maple whips beside a bubbling rivulet.

Luke fetched the woodcock back and dropped it in the palm of my hand. I smoothed the rumpled russet feathers, pulled a wet black leaf from its long, pink, flexible bill, and gently slid the plump, warm body into my game pocket.

Our fears were gone. From now on I could rest assured that these goofy, delightful little birds were a lot smarter and hardier than I'd thought. The nightmare was over.

D-DAY IN MARYLAND

Someone yells "mark!" and the season is underway. . . .

Three doves pour into the upper left-hand edge of the corn patch and begin a reconnaissance run down the strip of silage that bisects the field. Ragged blasts of gunfire chart their progress—two rapid pops from a 28-gauge double, then three deeper, more calculating chugs from a pump-action 12, followed by a fusillade of various gauges from most of the remaining guns scattered at forty-yard intervals along the field's perimeter.

For an instant I lose the birds in the shivering blur of sun glare and corn tassels behind my stand, but then they emerge, miraculously unscathed—three long gray blurs banking steeply

73

past the standing corn to my right, headed for safety in the lush green of the trees bordering the field's downhill slope. They're still out of range.

But nothing in dove hunting is certain.

Now the birds suddenly wheel back into the field, flaring from the edge of the covert to complete a full circle. They're boring straight for me, about forty feet high in the hazy blue air. I rise from one knee, the gun jumps to my shoulder as they sweep overhead—if this were a skeet range, they'd be perfect Station Eight birds. I fire and the leader puffs and falls, bouncing hard on the sunbaked stubble. For just an instant there, I'm batting a thousand on the new season. Keep it up and I just might limit out on half a box of shells. The trailing pair of doves are past me now, lining up just right for me to take both of them with the remaining shot in my double-barreled 20-gauge. I fire again . . . and miss them clean.

So much for a perfect season.

As the echoes fade and the heat of the day pounds ever hotter, cold reality settles down on the dove field. The birds are few and far between, coming mainly by twos and threes. By the time the sun sets over Chesapeake Bay, the twenty hunters in our party will have killed 142 birds—98 short of our legal limit. Not great shooting by any means but about typical for a dove opener with no great numbers of migrating birds on the move as yet. At day's end I count my empty shell cases, then my downed doves. Far more of the former than the latter: I've killed only seven birds with twenty-one shots. So okay, I'm batting .333. On any major league team I'd be a star. But dove hunting isn't baseball, and actually I've shot rather poorly.

Still (or so I console myself), success on the opening day of dove season—or of any game season, for that matter—isn't measured by body count. It's a day for the celebration of old passions once more rekindled, for the colors and aromas of impending autumn, for eager gundogs quivering at heel, their eyes scanning the skies for the wink of wings, their ears cocked for the whistle of primary feathers; for the gleam of fine guns in motion and the musk of burnt powder, the satisfying thud of four-ounce bodies hitting the ground and the soft drift of dove-down on the breeze. Mainly, though, it's a day for the renewal of old friendships in fine food, fast shooting, and, later, strong drink—the best time of the year for any wingshooter.

Doves are fair game in thirty-six states, and because dove season is usually the first to open each fall, it has taken on a symbolic, almost ritualistic quality as the harbinger of good things to come—especially in the mid-Atlantic and southern states, where it rivals the opening of the college football season, the Fourth of July, and even, in some places, Jefferson Davis's birthday for sheer hooraw and conviviality.

The opening of dove season is as close as we get in the United States to Britain's Glorious Twelfth—the tradition-steeped day in mid-August when Parliament takes a vacation and English sporting gentlemen are free to hunt grouse. It's also the closest thing we have to a classic English estate shoot, where the gunners stand waiting for the birds to fly over them and the socializing both before and after the shoot counts for as much as the bag itself. On both sides of the Atlantic, opening day is a time for young hunters to get started in the sport of wingshooting and for old men to fire their final shots. And because the mourning dove is a fast, erratic, and largely unpredictable target, the dove field on opening day is the best place I know to relearn humility, or at least to polish up rusty excuses for missed shots.

The mourning dove is the most abundant game bird in the country. As of 1990, the U.S. Fish and Wildlife Service estimated its continent-wide population at 475 million; doves outnumber people by nearly two to one. Only on their Western Flyway are the birds in a slight decline, due probably to the cutting of California's live oaks to make way for more suburban sprawl and thereby depriving doves of their preferred nesting sites. Another factor may be the planting of once-fallow ground in the vast San Joaquin Valley, a favored way station for doves on the seasonal move to cotton fields and nut groves. On the Central Flyway dove populations are on the increase, and in the East their numbers remain stable. West Coast dove limits were reduced to ten a day in 1987, while in the East they remain at twelve. In the Middle and Mountain West, you're allowed to kill fifteen doves a day if you're quick enough. Fish and Wildlife predicted that forty-five million doves would fall to gunners in 1990, more than twice as many as of America's sec-ond-most-harvested game bird, the bobwhite quail. So long as dove populations remain as high, healthy, and self-sustaining as they are now, there's no good reason why D (for Dove) Day should not remain a delightful American holiday for years to come.

I often celebrate D-Day at Joe Judge's Twin Ponds Duck Club, a 1,643-acre sprawl of dove fields, waterfowl marshes, and deer woods near Centreville on Maryland's Eastern Shore. Best known in sporting circles for his angling feats, Judge is a big, dark-bearded, middle-aged sportsman who's fished the waters of the world from Australia to Costa Rica, from Panama to the Bahamas to British Columbia, for world-record game fish on both heavy and light tackle. For a while he held the International Game Fish Association mark for tarpon in the 1-kilogram-line-test category with a 54-pound silver king caught in the Rio Colorado on Costa Rica's Caribbean coast. He's also landed many marlin in excess of a thousand pounds, most of them out of Cairns in Australia. When he's not fishing, Joe makes his home at Twin Ponds, one of the finest shooting establishments on the East Coast. The place reflects his taste for the best of what counts: good guns, good tackle, good dogs and food and drink. His longtime com-panion, Donna Davenport, is one of his finest choices. A short, vivacious outdoorswoman who loves to cook almost as much as she loves to fish, she currently holds three IGFA records, on jack crevalle (14 1/2 pounds on 2-kilo test), snook (27 1/2 pounds on 4-kilo), and tar-pon (83 pounds on 2-kilo). She's also a fine wingshot, as well as a crack deer hunter with both bow and black powder.

Dutifully enough, Donna was following a self-propelled lawn mower through tall grass near the lodge when I arrived two days before the dove season opened in 1990 on my first visit to Twin Ponds. She shut it off with a grin of gratitude and shook hands with a firm grip. "Thanks for the welcome interruption," she said.

I'd come down to the Shore from Vermont with my young yellow Labrador, Jake, who took an instant liking to Donna. While Jake unlim-bered from the long drive by engaging in a shouting match with Joe's kenneled Chesapeake Bay retrievers, Amigo and Maddie Hayes, I sized up the lodge. Contoured to the gentle landscape of the Eastern Shore, surrounded by sunflower, soybean, and feed-corn fields, it sits on a low bluff above the tidal waters of the Corsica River, which feeds into the Chester River and thence Chesapeake Bay itself. The silvery cedar-shake roof and slate blue siding blended nicely with the wraparound topography. A weathered wooden deck ran the length of the lodge overlooking the river, with a battery of foot-traps mounted along its railings. Boxes of clay pigeons and shotgun ammunition in all gauges stood ready at hand for the festivities to come.

Inside the lodge, where Joe was waiting for us, pine-paneled walls sloped airily upward to a skylit cathedral ceiling where big fans slowly stirred the air. A sunken lounge with a huge stone fireplace centered the long, burgundy-carpeted main room of the lodge. The west end of the room was the dining area, replete with long pine tables, comfortable easy chairs, and a kitchen dominated by a gleaming, industrial-strength Vulcan gas range, Donna's pride and joy.

One of the tables was devoted, during this season at least, to "gun stuff"—shell boxes, cleaning kits, bottles of solvent and gun oil, duck and goose calls, a few hand-carved basswood dove decoys, and, of course, gun cases. "Take a look at this," Joe said, opening one of them. "I think I'll shoot it on opening day." He pulled out a beautiful old Iver Johnson .410 side-by-side "Skeeter" with 30-inch barrels. The oil-finished walnut was superb. "I got it for nothing, almost," Joe said. "Swapped a goose blind for it."

At the other end of the main room was an amply stocked bar with Harp beer on tap. I washed down the road dust before taking a tour of the farm with Joe. "Got to feed my ducks," he said. "There are seven ponds on the property and I raise two or three hundred mallards on each of them. In addition to the base farm, I own or lease the shooting rights on a total of eight thousand acres. The pond-raised ducks help to toll in the flight birds. It keeps the gunning prime."

No doubt about it: The evidence was on the walls of the lodge—mount after mount of flighted waterfowl. Canada geese, snows, blues, canvasbacks, and redheads circled the interior walls in a seemingly nonstop skein, overseen by mounts of white-tailed deer and game fish, including snook, marlin, and sailfish frozen in the taxidermic time warp of midleap. At either end of the main room stood full-body mounts of a black bear and a South African bontebok, a small, colorful representative of the hartebeest family. On the wall behind the bar was pegged the hide of a record cinnamon-phase black bear that Joe killed while bow hunting in the arid country below New Mexico's Gila River. Broad-skulled and deep-piled, it glowed like old gold in the late-afternoon Chesapeake light.

While Donna prepared food for the opening-day festivities, we went out to look over the farm. Joe led the way in his pickup while I rode with his friend Rod Cawley in an open-topped, Afrika Korps–style *Kubelwagen,* actually a Volkswagen copy of the World War II Wehrmacht staff car produced in the early 1970s. Rod, a much-decorated cavalry recon trooper of the Vietnam War, is a decoy collector, wild turkey enthusiast, and guide in Joe's waterfowling operation.

First stop was the duck pond behind the barn where Joe stores his decoys and blinds. Some 360 barely fledged mallards walked up from the water's edge at the sound of Joe's truck, scrambling over one another's backs in their haste to get to the cascades of pelletized duck chow he poured for them. Four wild blue-winged teal circled warily over the far edge of the pond until we'd departed. From the duck pond we headed for the dove field, where Joe and Rod pounded in shooting boxes on the corn edges for the convenience of D-Day's gunners. They could lay open shell boxes on the shelves to make for speedier reloading. "This is a silage field," Joe said, "so you'll see a lot of waste corn lying on the ground. That's inevitable with modern harvesting techniques. But to make sure I'm legal I invite in the local game wardens to inspect the field we're going to shoot on opening day. I wouldn't want to be charged with baiting. So far it's always been kosher."

It was hot in the field, maybe 95 degrees, and hazily humid. Only a few doves were feeding at this hour. Others sat resting on the power lines overlooking the corn. "A big band of flight birds came in early this week," Joe said, "and I thought we were set for the opener. But they moved out the next day, probably across the river. You never know with dove. So I'm afraid that all we'll have to shoot at on opening day are the local birds who've been using these fields all summer. Still, there are plenty of them, mostly birds of the year who've never been shot at before. It could still be good shooting."

Toward sundown we drove over to one of Joe's bass ponds to exercise his largemouths on the fly rod. En route we passed a NO TRESPASSING sign where the road made a right-hand turn. Joe slowed to a crawl as we neared it. "Look at the center of the letter 'o,'" he said. As I did, a camera eye popped out and gazed at us. "That's the FBI's video camera. The Russian embassy owns a guesthouse—their 'dacha,' they call it—just down the road, and Big Brother likes to see who's coming to call. Smile, Pinko, you're on Candid Camera."

The bass were cooperative in the cooling dusk. Joe and I caught and released a pair of two-pounders apiece on deerhair bass bugs before the real bugs—mosquitoes the size of big mayflies—drove us off the water. There was still time and light enough back at the lodge to shoot some clay pigeons from the front-deck traps before Donna called us in to supper—spaghetti with venison sauce, garlic toast, and fresh green salad.

D-Day Minus One. We spent the morning out on the turbid brown water of the Corsica River running trotlines for the blue crabs that would serve as the mainstay of Donna's D-Day feast. We kept only the big crabs—"Number Ones" that measured at least $5\frac{1}{2}$ inches across the carapace. Actually Billy Foster did most of the crabbing. He's another of Joe's guides, a magnum-sized Eastern Shore waterman who measures, as Judge puts it, "about five-foot-twenty by 260 pounds." Foster's dexterity with the boat's helm and engines while he scooped crabs with a dip net from the three thousand trotlines would have awed a professional juggler. A hunk of eel was tied into the line every ten feet or so, and each piece seemed to have a crab clinging to it as it came to the murky surface. Billy had to decide in an instant if it was big enough to keep, then lean over and dip it just as the bait cleared the surface of the water and the crab dropped free. He'd flip the crab into the well of the boat before leaning over to inspect the next one, all the while keeping track of the boat's speed and direction and the presence of other potentially hazardous boat traffic on the swiftly flowing river. The blue crab's Linnean name is *Callinectes sapidus*, which means "beautiful swimmer, tasty." I'd read W. W. Warner's Pulitzer Prize–winning book, *Beautiful Swimmers,* about the Chesapeake watermen and their primary cash crop back in 1976 when it was published. Seeing Billy Foster in action made me realize that Warner hadn't exaggerated the skills of the waterman one bit.

That afternoon the mood of the weekend began to shift and pick up momentum. We began by fine-tuning the traps. A few clays thrown and shot at, then tighten the springs once again. A few more, then alter the deflection or elevation. All told we must have shot a hundred clays apiece before Judge was even partially satisfied. He tried my 20-gauge double, a Winchester Model 23 choked IC and modified, and pronounced it accurate but a bit heavy. I shot his guns, both the Johnson and a Pigeon Grade Browning 12-gauge, and pronounced them "wow!" Guests began to arrive with their guns and dogs. We adjusted the traps yet again, shot each others' guns, learned their histories, recalled good days and bad days afield, and shot some more—through case after case of Day-Glo orange clays, box after box of shells ranging from .410 to 10-gauge magnum. Joe's Gordon setter, MacGregor, peered wistfully from behind the glass of the deck door, and I could hear Jake howl now and then from his kennel. All this shooting, they seemed to say. It's not fair! We should be out there retrieving. . . . Their time would come.

D-Day broke cool and blue with a taste of midsummerlike humidity that wreathed the Shore in ground fog and promised a scorcher when the sun reached its zenith. Running with Jake up the crushed oystershell driveway on his morning outing, we flushed a few dozen doves from the roadway where they were dusting themselves and picking up grit for their crops, and more from the telephone wires. But there were no big concentrations of birds—no flocks that had miraculously appeared overnight like manna for the hungry Israelites. The shooting would be slow, I thought, coming in brief flurries, with a lot of time necessary to scratch down a limit. I've shot doves of various persuasions, from East Africa through southern Texas to Baja California, where the gunning was so fast and furious that you lost track of shell expenditure and body count. But I prefer a slower pace. It gives me a chance to savor each shot, to notice the details of the day—weather, wind, cloud patterns, the sky, perhaps a hungry hawk circling above the killing ground waiting to pick off a straggler. When groups of men are shooting, a slow day also gives me insights into the little nuances of shooting style that reveal character. Some men are whoopers and screamers—"Kee-yiii! Did you see me smoke that double?" By contrast, others are quiet with their successes, letting their guns do the talking. I guess I prefer them as shooting companions. Actually I'd much rather hunt alone. The presence of other men inevitably brings with it the specter of competition, which to my mind has no place in the hunting field.

The lodge was humming with activity by the time Jake and I got back from our morning run. The hiss and spatter of frying chicken competed with the chatter of late-arriving guests, along with the *boinggg* of springing traps, the bang of guns, the occasional plop of an unhit clay pigeon splashing into the river, and the raucous laughter at the guy who'd missed. Billy Foster arrived, having been up since 4 A.M., with three forty-pound baskets of Number One blue crabs. Transferring them to the steamer pots was a blood sport in itself. A big blue crab can take off a fingertip if you aren't careful, and these representatives of the species were mighty angry. Stuffing them into the pot, you have to have a quick hand with the tongs and a faster one with the lid to keep them from scrambling free. It's amazing how fast an ungainly crustacean can move when it's really motivated. Only by sprinkling the crabs with spicy "boil" could they be quieted.

Maryland allows early-season gunning on doves to run from noon to sunset, and with H-Hour fast approaching the furor of cooking and shooting reached a crescendo. A fellow named Billy Deoudes blazed away at multiple clay targets with an autoloader until the sky over the river was dotted black with what looked like flak puffs. Mike O'Harra shucked .410 rounds through his Remington Model 870, rarely missing. Another of Joe's friends, Dick Grizzard, bare-chested and skinny as a skeeterhawk, blasted three-inch .410s through a chrome-finished, rosewood-gripped Derringer, rarely hitting. Stuart Scharf arrived in his baby blue Rolls Royce, puffing a fat stogie, then cracked jokes and clays simultaneously. Then dinner was served—Maryland fried chicken, coleslaw, sliced tomatoes, and pot after pot of steaming, brick red, succulent beautiful swimmers. Gunfire and conversation ceased. The only sounds to be heard were the tapping of wooden mallets on crab claws, the crunch of crisp chicken wings, and a low mutter of approval. Even Ed Cook and Bernard Dadds, the Maryland game wardens who'd come by at Joe's request to inspect the fields and give a brief safety lecture to the shooters, were grinning like civilians.

That mood of contentment prevailed throughout a long, hot, slow afternoon of so-so shooting. It would get better later in the season when the flight birds moved through the area, when thirty guns could drop limits of 360 birds in an hour. But there were high points enough on this particular opening day: Joe's neighbor Dick Quillman folding a high-passing dove with his H&H 12-bore "best gun" so that it bounced neatly at his feet; some hotshot in the far corner of the field smoking a trio of midafternoon birds while another guy down the line yelled, "Hey, it's raining doves out here!" A few of the fellows played war games, lobbing corncobs at one another like hand grenades when the action lagged. Others stripped to the waist, snoozing as they worked on their tans. Now and then came the welcome sound of Joe's pickup or Rod Cawley's *Kubelwagen* making the rounds with iced soft drinks.

Jake and I got our share of the action, though. It was his first time in a dove blind and he behaved well—no yipping or barking. He sat calmly beside me as the birds came over and I stood to shoot, marking them down with his grave brown eyes if they dropped, then waiting for my hand signal to bound out and pick them up. One bird fell into the second-growth jungle of grapevines and catbriers beyond the corn, but he weaseled right on in there without a whimper and emerged a minute later with the dove held lightly in his grinning jaws, his eyes bright with triumph. He dropped it neatly at my feet, circled once or twice, then sat again, steady as a rock, waiting for more.

So there was shooting enough, and meat on the ground when the sun went down at 7:38 P.M. Back at the lodge, Donna breasted the doves for broiling. Joe set up and lit off a fireworks barrage on the riverbank lawn, drawing *oohs* and *aahs* from the sailboats anchored offshore in the deepening blue dusk. Then the traps began to *twang* once more and the merry sound of gunfire filled the eventide. Yes, I thought, D-Day.

We'd gotten the season off to a bangup start. But the real beauty of any opening day is that, like a kid on the cusp of summer vacation, you can look ahead to a whole long string of seemingly endless weeks lying just ahead—days of bleak gray skies, biting winds, frost-burned alders, and shivering popples in the grouse and woodcock coverts; of sweet, gnarled apples plucked from old upland orchards; of ducks cupping into the decoys from an angry, racing sky, or pheasants rattling up from the swamp edge, the dogs still locked on point in the golden light of a late autumn afternoon. All of it, over and over again—all of it yet to come.

A DOG'S BEST FRIEND

The clamor is faint at first, querulous and questioning as they lift off the river half a mile away, then louder as the flock nears the set. There is no music on earth quite so thrilling. Jake lifts his heavy, anvil-shaped head from my knee and searches the sky. He knows this sound means impending action, but can he in some mysterious way also understand the aerial dialogue? He's a Labrador, so I wouldn't be a bit surprised.

Louder, closer, losing altitude now as they circle, all their yammer drowns out thought—but it's becoming "happy talk" as the geese let their appetites take charge. Unmistakable, that sound:

a confident, anticipatory chatter as the Canadas assure one another that everything will be dandy once they've touched down.

But in the dark, dank pit-blind, tension mounts. The dog is shivering uncontrollably now, his eyes rolled skyward toward the light that filters in through small gaps in the camouflage. This is a critical moment. If Jake yips only once, the geese might flare off. Shadows flicker over us, big ones, accompanied by the winnowing sound of strong wings hissing overhead. Jake is pressing himself tight and hot against my leg. Joe Judge, my host and shooting partner, wisely refrains from any further calling. It's the last weekend of the season, and at such close range the slightest sour note could turn the flock away from us. Joe's eyes, too, are straining upward, waiting for that final moment when the flock sets its wings in commitment to the spread. My hand is tight on the lever that controls the sliding roof of the pit-blind. Like Jake, I'm shivering—but not from the cold.

"*Now!*"

I yank the lever and the roof whooshes open. Suddenly we're on our feet, guns swinging automatically to our shoulders, unwilled, without thought.

The sky is solid, swirling Canadas—caught with their flaps down.

I swing on a big gander, his black paddles spread downward for the landing, beady eyes bright black, his pale gray breast roseate in the sunrise light—then check my swing at the last moment. *Too tough to chew*—my first conscious thought in twenty minutes. Instead I switch over to a younger bird vainly struggling to regain flight speed, primaries spread like fingers to claw at the frosty air—*bam!* The triplex load— T-BB-2—smacks home dead center. The bird folds and thuds to the frozen earth, bounces once in the dry corn stubble, and lies still. Joe's Browning A5 bellows at the far end of the blind. *Click-clack!* I see the glint of brass and red plastic as he shucks an empty, then I'm swinging smoothly with the 12-gauge Beretta over-and-under on a goose that's almost back to speed, moving away from me at a slight left-to-right angle of deflection. From the edge of my vision I see Joe swing on another bird, off to the far left. We fire simultaneously—both birds topple and bounce. We look at each other and smile, eyes locked and happy.

Jake is standing on the bench, solemn and hot-eyed, watching me for the signal. I swing my hand outward.

"Fetch 'em, boy!"

He's out of the pit like a blond muzzle blast—a big, strong, pantherine dog doing what he was born to do. He pays no heed to the stuffers and silhouettes arrayed cannily around the pit. His eyes seek only the downed birds, the real thing. He runs past the first one—a single glance tells him it's stone dead, not going anywhere, he can fetch it later. Farther out a goose is still struggling in the cornstalks about forty yards from the blind. He scoops it up at a run, hardly slowing at all, turns on a dime (leaving nine cents change), and shifts the big bird in his wide-stretched mouth so that it balances evenly from his grip across its back. Head high, tail wagging, he gallops back to where I'm standing, still in the blind. He drops the goose right in front of me— *kerthunk!*—and turns to run left, toward Joe's birds.

In that moment I swear that he winks at me, then grins as he runs off to finish the job.

It would be gratifying to say I taught him all of that—his steady, silent discipline in the blind, his eagerness to retrieve, his knowledge of which birds to deal with first once they're on the ground, and the uncanny ability to mark all the downed birds the instant he's out of the blind. But the more I hunt, whether in the uplands or for waterfowl, the more I'm convinced that the most important element in the making of a good gundog is not hard-core force training inspired by fear, but rather a constant, almost symbiotic companionship fueled by the dog's innate desire to please.

This will be Jake's fourth season, and already he's the best gundog I've ever owned. Through the years—more than forty seasons—I've hunted over setters, Brittanies, German shorthairs, Chessies, and a whole laboratory of Labs, but never one so quick to learn. It sometimes seems to me that Jake didn't have to learn at all: He knew it all from the moment he saw a shotgun.

The irony is that Kent Hollow Jake, to give him his proper A.K.C. name, comes almost entirely from bench stock. I live in Vermont but got him from a breeder in Zeeland, Michigan, at the suggestion of a friend who'd recently lost his nonhunting yellow Labrador bitch and thought it would be nice if we both had pups from the same litter.

Like most hunters, I was leery of yellow Labs, which are bred primarily for show. Most of my previous experience had been with black Labs from field bloodlines. I'd had a yellow Lab years earlier, a big, hardheaded dog named Simba who'd been only fair-to-middling in the field, eager enough and a radar-nosed retriever but hardmouthed much of the time. I mainly hunted the northeastern uplands in those days. Grouse, woodcock, and pheasant were our stock in trade, and Simba always insisted on crunching the first bird of the season—often the last as well, and maybe a few in the middle. But then, I'd picked him up almost haphazardly when he was already a year and a half old, from a British couple who were moving back to Blighty and didn't want to subject the dog to the long imprisonment of quarantine required by British immigration law. I had a good gundog at the time—a German shorthair named Max—and figured that the addition of a full-time retriever to our hunting team would do no harm.

Twenty years later, I once again had a good gundog, a black Lab named Luke with a multichampion field background. I'd trained him from puppyhood on both upland birds and ducks, and he could literally read my mind. But Luke had worked hard all his life and when he was eleven years old, I knew he only had a couple more seasons in him at best. Perhaps if I got a pup while Luke was still hunting, the old dog could teach the pup a few subtle things that were beyond my all-too-paltry human skills. Maybe he could even teach a *yellow* Lab how to hunt!

It was worth a try.

We started Jake on upland birds the first day he arrived at his new home. He was still wobbly on his outsized paws, but Luke's keen spirit struck a spark in the pup that quickly blazed to a five-alarm fire. Before he was three months old, Jake was flushing woodcock regularly and even a partridge or two. Luke kept a lock on all the retrieving chores, though. Only in his second season would the older dog allow the pup to fetch.

Jake had been whelped in August, so I didn't start him on water-fowl until that second season when he was just over a year old. By then he'd already become a fine flushing dog, but I worried that as a result of all the fast-moving upland work, he'd be restless in a blind—one of Luke's few faults. The old dog was such a charger that he often whined and fidgeted in a blind, sometimes even yipping uncontrollably just as ducks or geese were about to pitch in. He always looked properly guilty after he'd done so, but he just couldn't help himself, nor could I break him of the fault. Fearful that Luke would transmit this bad habit to Jake (even as he'd already transmitted so many good ones), I regretfully left the old dog at home that year when I went down to Joe Judge's place for the early duck season—Jake's first.

Joe's Twin Ponds Duck Club is one of the finest waterfowl venues I've ever had the pleasure to shoot. Countless ducks—some of them returnees from the twenty-five thousand mallards Judge has banded and released over the years—and up to a quarter of a million Canada geese use the immediate area during the fall and winter. In an era marked by increasingly woeful waterfowl shooting on the Atlantic Flyway, Judge has managed through canny habitat improvement and judicious man-agement to retain much of the richness of the area's legendary past.

Well before sunup the next day, Joe parked his truck at the edge of the Chester River and we hiked through the dark with Jake at heel. Wind from the north at thirty knots. Spartina thrashed and surf boomed on the rocks, sloshing and foaming at our feet—cold as the gunmetal dawn just breaking. Jake had never seen a johnboat before but he jumped right in at my command. The blind too, when we got there, seemed as familiar to him as our living room back home. It was as if he'd been there many times before, and perhaps he had been, some-where in the depths of the wondrous Labrador gene pool.

Luckily, action came quickly that morning. Too long a wait might have made Jake fidget. Across the bay I saw a raft of ducks lift skyward into the first light for their breakfast feed. "Get ready," Joe said. "Here they come." He began to call. . . .

Jake perked his ears at the strengthening gabble of duck talk, the whistle of wings getting louder as the flight approached. Luke might have been whining and yipping by now, unable to control himself. But the young dog lay steady, only his shiver betraying the excitement he felt. Even his eyebrows were shivering. But he kept his head down, eyes averted almost purposely from the first ducks—greenheads and baldpates—that slashed overhead and circled back into the dekes. I looked up and saw them, cupped for the touchdown. We rose and opened fire. . . .

When the smoke cleared and I opened the door of the blind, Jake was out like a shot. He'd seen the angles we'd been shooting at and stared out over the water to mark the fallen ducks. At Joe's hand signal, he hit the water with a long, leaping splash and swam strongly through weed and breaking waves—pausing only once to grab at a decoy, which he quickly rejected (and he never bothered a decoy again). All told, Jake brought in twenty-five ducks that weekend, both for us and for others hunting Joe's water. He handled cripples as deftly and gently as he did dead birds, unlike some retrievers who use a crip's thrashing as an excuse to hardmouth it.

Later in the season, when we came down for geese, I witnessed his first confrontation with a big, broken-winged honker. The gander stood taller than Jake, hissing as formidably as a king cobra, one wing extended in a clublike threat display. Jake studied the bird for a moment, feinted to his left, then ducked around to the right behind the goose and grabbed it by the root of its good wing. That was a tactical error, as he soon learned, because as he brought it into the field blind, its dragging weight pulled him around in a series of awkward loops. We went out and showed him how to grasp the bird across the back, pinning its wings to its sides, a lesson he's never forgot.

"You've got a good dog," Joe said—high praise indeed.

Jake was bred for looks, not hunting ability. How then can I account for his considerable talents in the field and, more significantly, the speed with which he learned to use them? Was his keenness to hunt already there when I got him, immersed in his bloodlines, or was he motivated to hunt by contact (and perhaps competition) with Luke? As to tactics, Luke certainly taught him a lot—but only about upland game. How did he get so smart so fast when we got around to waterfowl?

I firmly believe it's a Labrador's innate desire to please that makes him such a quick study. No other breed, in my experience, is quite so playful, quite so eager to learn the games its master plays, or quite so happy when he gets it all right. If that's true, then my instinctively laid-back, low-key training methods, developed over years of gundog ownership, have added up to the correct regimen.

I've spent long hours with Jake right from the start at such "games" as obedience, retrieving, and actual bird hunting.

I talk to him a lot so that he recognizes my tones of voice—praiseful, warning, remonstrative, excited, good-humored, or commonsensical.

I maintain eye contact with him as much as I can—he now feels the "weight" of my gaze even when his back is to me. He watches me in turn; and from my unconscious body-language and facial expressions, he has learned to anticipate most of my wishes.

When he does what I want, I reinforce what I've taught him with lavish praise and plentiful petting. A dog can't get enough of that stuff.

I try to anticipate his thought processes and his next move, distracting him if it's something I don't want him to do, encouraging him if it is.

If I'm seated somewhere and he's beside me, which inevitably he is, I'll reach down from time to time even when I'm doing something else and pat his head, grab him by the muzzle, and let him chew on my fingers, warning him with a growled "no!" if his jaws close too tightly. Thus he's learned to be soft-mouthed when he picks up something that "belongs" to me, whether it's my hand or a duck I've shot.

As a result of this mutual attention we pay one another, I can literally read his mind and he's learned to read mine. In short, I've become my dog's best friend and I never let him forget it. Any dog owner should try it, whether he hunts or not.

THE TODD SEEBOHM SAGA

The first thing you see on entering Joe Judge's Twin Ponds Duck Club is the mount of a 511-pound blue marlin, caught by Joe himself during a tournament at Orange Beach, Alabama, back in 1983. Over the bar at one end of the long main room hangs the pegged pelt of a cinnamon bear, and on the floor, grimacing testily next to a Dolly Parton pinball machine, stands the full-body mount of a black bear. The tall-tined heads of trophy whitetails gaze philosophically from the walls, but most intriguing to a bird hunter are the birds, frozen forever in midflight: Canadas, blues, and snow geese—known snugly as "snoogies" here on the Eastern Shore.

"Gee," said my hunting partner, Todd Seebohm, fourteen, "all those dead things—that's *cool!*"

Todd is the grandson of my nearest neighbor in Vermont, and though he lives way down in New Jersey, he visits her often. I've known him since he was born, shortly after my wife and I moved to Vermont. When he was about six or seven, he started hanging around my place, enthralled by the guns and fly rods in my study (less so by my too-huge collection of hunting and fishing books, though lately he's started to read them). What hunter can resist a kid like that? I bought a Daisy Red Ryder BB gun and taught him to shoot. I taught him well, as I had my own kids when they were Todd's age, and soon I could trust him to plink away safely at old coffee cans without my supervision. I also taught him to fly cast. Pretty quickly he was catching brook trout and panfish in the nearby ponds and streams—though only occasionally releasing them. Kids are by nature game hogs, and the instinct is hard to overcome.

But it was guns that had Todd's full attention. In short order, I was letting him shoot at clays with an old Savage .22/.410 over-and-under of mine. Then with a 20 gauge Winchester Model 23. I taught him to swing through and shoot without stopping. By the time he was twelve he was smoking the clays.

Todd's "Nana," a cheerful woman named Ruth Moore, now in her eighties but still an active hiker, canoeist, naturalist, and gardener, found a battered old 16-gauge Fox she'd inherited from her father, with which she used to hunt pheasants and quail. Todd started shooting the Fox. He was a natural. Then his parents remembered an ancient 12-gauge Remington Model 11 autoloader, built on the Browning patents, that another great-grandfather had been wont to go a-ducking with, and Todd moved up in the world.

It took a lot of persuading on my part, boys being boys, to get Todd to enroll in a hunter safety course down in New Jersey and thereby qualify for a hunting license, but finally he did it, scoring better than 90 percent on the written exam and actually busting clays when his instructor threw them for the class. "I was the only guy to hit one," Todd told me later, not without a smirk of pride. As a reward for his assiduity—he hates to study—I promised him a trip to my pal Joe Judge's place, on Maryland's legendary Eastern Shore, for his first-ever goose hunt.

All the way down there—a hectic eight-hour drive during the week between Christmas and New Year's—he kept asking, "How much farther is it? When will get there? What's it going to be like? Do you think I'll actually kill a goose? Gosh I hope I do. Are they any good to eat, how do you clean them, where will we hunt?" He was more excited than Jake, who sat beside me in the front seat like a veteran long-haul trucker.

As we turned south from Middletown onto Maryland 301, we started seeing geese—at first just small skeins of Canadas trading from field to field at midday under an ominous overcast, then a solid acre of snoogies milling on the ground in a soybean field. Little clots of mallards and great knots of divers rafted on the rivers and estuaries we crossed, or buzzed through the lowering gray sky in that thrilling high dudgeon that seems to infect the duck clan.

"Mister Jones, how much should I lead them when I shoot?"

"Hey, just swing through your bird fast, like I taught you. Always pick a specific bird, never shoot into the 'brown.' And you can call me 'Bob.' We're hunting partners now."

"Okay, Mister Bob."

"I wonder how much that kid's going to sleep tonight?" Joe said when Todd toddled off to bed that night, after a hearty supper of prime venison with all the fixin's.

"Not a wink," laughed Donna Davenport, Joe's lady, a world-class sportswoman in her own right and the author of that fine meal.

"The shooting's been great," Joe said. "More birds than I've seen in a long while." And indeed there were. During the afternoon we'd driven around Joe's farm along the Corsica River, past fields loaded with feeding Canadas, the river itself crisscrossed with seemingly supersonic flights of divers—redheads, canvasbacks, blackheads, and of course the ubiquitous but virtually inedible ruddies. At sunset the geese had returned from the fields to the water, and Todd's eyes had widened at their sky-obscuring abundance. Their clamor had filled the air, louder and far lovelier than even teenage rock 'n' roll.

"There must be ten thousand Canadas using in this immediate area," Joe reckoned. I didn't doubt him. I rarely do.

Todd was staying in a bedroom adorned with the mounts of Canada geese and a rare (for those parts) specklebelly that had been killed by Joe's good friend Ray Arnett, a controversial Undersecretary of the Interior during the Reagan era. Ray's a big, genial, outspoken Californian, a consummate hunter and overall sportsman, and I hoped that some of his karma would rub off on Todd by sympathetic magic.

He was up bright-eyed and bushy-tailed at four the next morning, rarin' for breakfast and ready to bust caps. Daylight broke blustery and near-zero cold, with divers trading along the river and coming in from Chesapeake Bay in unbelievable numbers. Great weather for waterfowl hunters. The first flights of geese were lifting off as we pulled on our boots and camo gear, grabbed our cased shotguns, and headed out in Joe's truck for Possum Point, across the Corsica from the lodge. There was a taste of snow on the air—a promise that would develop into a full-scale blizzard by that afternoon.

While Joe and guide Dan Lovely arranged stuffers near our field blind, Todd and I got settled inside, along with Jake. Todd had recently bought a puppy from one of the litters Jake had sired, and had named his dog "Luke," after my own great black Lab, who had taught Jake all he knew. We hadn't been able to bring the new Luke along on this trip, but I promised Todd we would next year. As we waited, I explained the strategy of Joe's decoy layout—the birds head-on or nearly so to the wind, the "hole" left in the spread to allow real geese to settle in within shooting range.

"When the geese come and Dan says 'get ready,' be sure to keep your face down," I said. "Watch Dan's eyes. They'll tell you where the birds are. Nothing spooks geese worse at the last moment than the flash of white faces looking up from a blind. Don't look at them except from the tops or the corners of your eyes. When Dan says 'take 'em!' I want you to stand up, pick your bird, swing the gun, and kill it. Center it. Just kill it stone dead. . . .

"And listen," I told him as he started to shiver a bit, "no matter how cold it gets, no matter how slow the shooting is—and we may not get any at all, it happens that way sometimes—don't you *ever* be the first one to suggest going home. One of the things about waterfowl hunting, it's about suffering in silence. Get it?"

"Got it," Todd said.

"Good."

But I realize now that he wasn't shivering from the cold. He was shivering with pent-up excitement. How could a boy—or an old man like me for that matter—not be excited on such a day, with the sky singing goose songs above the black water and the frozen plowground, a celestial chorus of strong, hot, close-feathered birds pelting up and down the river and across the fields as the light strengthens and the blood gets up?

"They're coming in from the water," Dan whispered from his vantage point at the right end of the blind. "Headed our way."

He and Joe worked their calls—*aaankh-ah, aaankh-ah, ahnk-ahnk-ahnk*—and I could see Todd watching Dan's eyes as they followed the birds in toward us. Now Jake, knowing what was coming from long experience, was shivering hot against my legs.

"They're going to do it! They're doing it! Get ready!"

I saw Todd strip the glove from his trigger hand, grip the throat of his great-grandfather's Remington, place his fingertip on the trigger-guard safety, and shiver some more.

"Almost here, almost here," Dan said, hunkering lower in the blind. "They're over the standing corn. Circling, circling . . ."

We could hear the winnowing beat of heavy wings overhead and see their faint shadows flash across the floor of the blind.

"Okay, they're cupping in—cupping in—legs out. . . . *Get 'em!*"

We stood as one man. The sky before us was black and white and gray with geese, caught with their wings down. As I raised my own gun, I saw Todd swing up, lock his cheekbone against the Remington's comb, his eyes blazing. *Wham!*—and then it was all gunfire and shell cases spinning through the cold clear air and geese falling *thump* on the ground, feathers wafting earthward, and Jake hot against my leg, shivering himself to pieces. I'd seen Todd's first goose crumple and fall, centered, and bounce on the frozen field.

"Good shooting, kid," Joe said when the bird lay still. He stuck out his hand. Todd looked over, an embarrassed grin trying to break on his face, and shook hands all around.

"You sure rolled that goose, Todd," Dan said. "Rolled him stone dead. Great shooting, m' man!"

"I told you he could shoot," I said. "I taught him."

"Okay, that's four down," Joe said, all business again. "Let's get Jake out there and bring 'em in fast. There's more coming any second now, and we've got another four to go for our limit."

Jake was out of the door in a flash, bringing dead geese back lickety-split. Then he took off after a runner. The big gander pecked at him when Jake tried to grab it, batted the big Lab with his wings. Jake wisely backed off and looked to us for help. The nip of a big male Canada can smart some. Dan finished the bird with a headshot and Jake brought it in.

We sat for ten minutes, grinning, then another toll came in. Once again Todd shot well. I could see it in his eyes, in the way he stood with his back straight, leaning forward a bit into the recoil, his eyes locked on his bird as it bucked to the shot string, and fell.

That filled our limit.

We were back at the lodge before noon. Outside it was snowing hard, with both the barometer and the temperature falling as fast as the geese of that morning. Split oak blazed in the big stone fireplace and we sat in front of it, cleaning our weapons, sipping hot coffee, talking about guns and game birds and hunts gone by, telling the old stories that hunters have told since the days when we all dressed in bearskins. Todd's eyes were shining, but they were full of confidence. For better or worse, he was one of us now. . . .

"**W**hat did you think of it?" I asked him as we drove home three days later, with our geese packed in the coolers on the rear deck of my Trooper and another eight hours of interstate ahead of us.

"It was cool," Todd said cautiously. At his age, in this era, a boy doesn't gush. Then, after a long pause—"Joe's way cool. So's Dan. So's Donna. How much money would I have to save to buy a cool place like Joe's?"

"A cool million for openers," I said. "You'd better get started right away."

Oh yes, he's ruined, I thought to myself. Ruined for sure.

Just like the rest of us.

FURTHER ADVENTURES OF TODD

The year after Todd Seebohm's first goose hunt, we went down to Joe Judge's farm near Centreville once again, this time to see if Todd could bag his first-ever white-tailed deer, and to get in some bird hunting at the same time. My own passion for deer hunting has long since abated. I get bored very quickly on a deer stand, and shooting things from ambush has always struck me as faintly ignoble. I prefer to move fast and loose through woods and fields and swamps, preferably behind a gundog of my own training, to hear and feel and see the birds flush up close and personal, all of it happening in an instant, and then to watch the dog make a stylish retrieve if I've hit what I was firing at. But of course young boys are heartless killers, bloodthirsty as the day is long, the manner of the hunt is immaterial to them, and the bigger the animal they can knock down, the better in their book. We all have to go through that phase, I guess.

Todd was now fifteen. Weedlike, he'd grown about four or five inches during the intervening year, his voice was changing, and he sported a full complement of facial zits as well as the wispy beginnings of a mustache. Few things in nature are quite as repulsive as a boy in the first throes of puberty. But what the hell, he was my friend and my hunting partner—in a way my ersatz grandson, in the absence (for the moment at least) of the real item. Neither of my own children has yet produced offspring. With no blood kin to spoil, I'd taught Todd to shoot and to fish and infected him with a love of fine guns, elegant fly rods, the smells of burnt powder and freshly killed meat, and the rough cama-raderie of hunting and fishing camps. I could put up with his passage through the "awkward age."

On the long drive down to Joe's we talked about football, wrestling (Todd's on his high school's team in both of those sports), politics (he's an incipient conservative, just like me), and babes (he's got a girlfriend now, though he wouldn't tell me her name—true gentleman that he is). The Eastern Shore is shotgun country for deer, and I'd advised Todd well in advance to sight in his 12-gauge Remington Model 11 autoloader with plenty of rifled slugs, shooting from various angles and a steady rest at ranges varying from twenty-five to seventy-five yards. That way he'd learn how his smoothbore threw. But—typically for a teenage boy—he'd done so only at the last minute, firing just a few paltry rounds at a crude paper target some fifty yards away, and his "group"—which he showed me—was random to say the least. Well, he'd learn. . . .

As we wheeled into Joe's Pioneer Point Farm on the Corsica River at dusk, the sky was loud and black with Canada geese returning from the corn and soybean fields to the water where they'd raft for the night. But geese wouldn't open for a while yet, and the early duck season had come and gone. The only birds we could hunt legally right now were quail and doves.

There were plenty of deer though. They'd already emerged that evening from the swamps and oak woods to feed in the stubble fields, and we counted at least a hundred plump does and a spike buck or two on the half-mile drive into camp. Todd's eyes lit up. Easy pickin's. . . .

"I've got too many does on the place," Joe told us when we'd settled ourselves in the lodge. "So feel free to cull one if you want—preferably a big, fat, barren doe if you can manage it. They eat too much and drive the younger, reproductive deer away from the best feeding grounds. But if you see a decent buck, take him." By "decent" he meant eight points or better.

"All I want's a deer of any kind," Todd said. "Horns don't matter." Well, he'd learn.

"How's the quail crop?" I asked.

"Plenty of 'em," Joe said. "You can go out with Peter Scheaffer if you want, during the middle of the day when the deer aren't moving."

Peter has a put-and-take quail and pheasant operation just west of Joe's farm. Originally from Cape Cod, where he'd been a commercial fisherman, he's a loquacious yarn spinner and a first-rate trainer of pointing dogs. Todd had never hunted quail and I was curious to see his reaction to a covey rise—the dazzling brown blur that quickly sorts the men from the boys.

We spent the following morning, from first light to 11 A.M., in a portable tree stand at Possum Point, another farm Joe owns just across the river from the lodge. I wasn't hunting, merely advising. Nothing was moving but geese and squirrels. The stand was in a red oak grove on the edge of the same cornfield where Todd had killed his first geese the previous year. We amused ourselves by watching the gray squirrels chasing each other through the treetops, Todd giggling whenever one of them fell unhurt to the loud leaves below.

At about 10:30 I heard deer moving toward us through the underbrush to the south and nudged Todd's shoulder. I pointed. A big doe and three yearlings emerged at a trot from the woods and ran into the cornfield. They stopped, looking back the way they'd come.

I estimated the range at seventy-five yards. The shot was just possible for a man who was confident of his shotgun, who'd fired it often enough to lob a slug into a six-inch circle over the heart/lung area at that distance. But this lad wasn't that man. He hadn't shot enough in practice yet and would probably miss the doe entirely, or—worse—gut shoot her. When he looked at me, pleading for permission to shoot, I shook my head firmly. "No."

"If you'd only wounded her," I told him later, "she'd have been across that corn piece in a dozen jumps and into the swamp before we could get down from the stand. Then we'd have to track her out along her blood trail, and the tracking conditions with all these red leaves on the ground would be miserable. Chances are we'd lose her, and that's no way to start your deer hunting career. When we get back to Joe's, I want you to fire at least a box of slugs through your gun, at that target he has in the sideyard—make sure you know how it shoots."

That afternoon we went over to Peter Scheaffer's and, after listening to a rambling but exciting account of various Cape Cod fishing misadventures, hit the quail fields. The birds here had already been shot at and missed, had spent a week or more surviving on their own, and would therefore be a bit sportier than freshly planted quail. A big fellow named John Whaley, who trains for Scheaffer, would guide us. He was working with a German shorthair pointer named Macha, not a puppy but a mature bitch, who had a tendency to break point when birds flushed and go haring off after them. John had a shock collar on her. Macha looked familiar to me, and later I learned that I'd met her before—in Costa Rica, of all places. She belonged to Bill Barnes, who owns and operates the Casa Mar tarpon lodge on the Rio Colorado, where I'd fished a few years earlier. Billy is a good friend of Joe's and a frequent visitor, hence the connection.

A drainage ditch flanked the soybean field where Macha hit her first point. I went in and a single got up—I mounted the gun too quickly and lunched the bobwhite dead center. Nothing left but beak and claws and matted pulp.

"That's *not* the way to do it," I told Todd. "I should have let the bird get farther out, to open up the pattern more. You take the next one."

Farther along the bean patch Macha locked up again, head low and intent, staring down into the dry stalks.

"Walk in just ahead of where she's looking," I told Todd. "Walk fast and scuffle your feet. These are pen-raised birds and they're reluctant to fly. Don't try to spot them on the ground—just keep walking. When they get up, don't shoot into the brown. Pick your bird, kill it, then pick another."

This time five birds went up—that low, buzzing, starshell burst that jumpstarts the heart and brings the gun up automatically. Todd had listened to my advice. He waited a beat or two after the flush, until the birds were twenty yards out, then mounted his gun and hit the trigger. A bobwhite puffed and folded, thumping down into the beans. He fired again—a miss this time. It would have been too much to expect a double on the first quail flush of his life.

"I think you've got it," I told him nonetheless. "Well done."

We shook hands, and Todd tried to control his grin.

Alternating points and shots, we killed another eight or ten birds over the next half hour. It was quick shooting, and Macha held her points so staunchly that John didn't have to use the shock collar more than two or three times. The afternoon was cool with a low autumn sun glowing richly golden through the tidewater haze as we walked the rustling beanfields. I thought again of how gentle quail hunting can be. Flat ground, easy walking, plenty of time to get up to the point; no ducking under grapevines or pushing through alder hells and briers or pounding uphill and down with your heart in your throat as in ruffed grouse or woodcock hunting. Of course it would be better if these quail were truly wild. They'd fly faster, for one thing, and probably display more tactical sense in their flight patterns—zipping out low and quick toward the cover of flanking trees and brush. But still, these pen-raised bobwhites were tight-holding and forgiving, perfect for a boy's introduction to the joys of wingshooting. The hard stuff could come later, and I was sure that in Todd's case it would. That smile had said it all.

The following morning, hunting with a client of Joe's named Jack Deurer—an inveterate Pennsylvania deer hunter with more enthusiasm for the game than I can now muster—Todd got his first deer. A 120-pound doe at about thirty yards in mixed beech and oak woods: one shot, down and dead.

"Come on, babe," Todd said as he prepared to drag her out of the woods, "you're my date for tonight."

AMERICA'S BIRD

In the
early days of
this grand
republic,
the North
American
wild turkey
ranged in
greater or
lesser numbers over three-quarters of the nation
and well down into Mexico. So tasty was the
bird that Benjamin Franklin—statesman and
trencherman *extraordinaire*—nominated it on
culinary grounds alone as our national bird. But
by the beginning of this century, thanks to market
gunning and ruinous logging practices, wild
turkeys were nearly extinct. On the eve of World
War II, only about thirty thousand remained—
most of them in the South and Southwest.

For a while, state wildlife agencies with the help of local rod and gun clubs tried restocking with pen-raised birds, but it didn't work. These half-tame turkeys were happier in a barnyard than the big woods, fell easy prey to predators, and died in droves during hard winters. Not until the development of the cannon-propelled capture net in the 1960s did game managers have a tool for live-trapping mature wild turkeys and planting them in suitable habitat elsewhere. The slow return of eastern farmlands to second-growth forest enhanced the process. In Vermont, not ten miles from where I live, an initial planting in 1968 of thirty-one birds from New York State thrived so well that a spring gobbler season was opened five years later. The rest of New England, from Maine to Connecticut, was stocked with relocated birds over the next few years, while similar restoration programs were succeeding all across the country.

Today, huntable populations of America's premier game bird—more than two million all told—exist in every state but Alaska. You can even hunt them in Hawaii. The return of the wild turkey is one of the greatest wildlife success stories of the twentieth century.

What's more, it occurred to me recently, turkey hunting is good for our souls—just about the most politically correct thing you can do in today's gender-sensitive America. In fact, it beats mountain biking, whitewater rafting, Roller Blading, and even fly fishing as a with-it sport for the '90s. How can this be? Simple. More than any other outdoor endeavor you can name, the pursuit of wild spring gobblers brings out a man's feminine side.

How do we go about reducing that great big gorgeous galoot to our exclusive possession?

Well, first we put on makeup and/or a veil, and dress up in a cunning new outfit carefully chosen to match the colors of our surroundings. Then we go out in the spring woods, warblers trilling all around us, in hopes of a torrid assignation. We pose seductively against a tree and commence to work our girlish wiles. Clucks and whines, whistles and purrs, yelps and cutts.

Come on, Big Guy, I'm yours for the taking.

Then, when the Big Guy finally comes sauntering over, no doubt with date rape on his mind, we let him have it smack in the kisser—with a buffered load of No. 5s.

Susan Faludi would love it.

Indeed, there've been a few times, during the rapid onrush of a testosterone-crazed gobbler, when I've feared for my own virginity. . . .

But let's get serious. The more I think about it, the more I'm convinced that scouting is the most important ingredient to success in hunting the North American wild turkey. It's even more important—though barely—than knowing how to talk turkey. You have to know where those birds are roosting if you're going to get a shot the next morning.

Just walking through the woods hoping to spot a gobbler won't do it. A turkey can see or hear you long before you'll be aware of his presence. Going into the woods before dawn, then sitting and listening for tree-yelps or wake-up gobbles won't do it, either, unless you're lucky enough to have set up by chance near a roosting tree. Unless you can stalk as silently and unobtrusively as a house cat, the moment you begin to move in on a distant gobbler the odds against your success rise ruinously.

Your best bet is to "roost" the birds the evening before you hunt. Male turkeys will sound off with territorial gobbles when they bed down for the night, sometimes for twenty minutes or more. An hour at dusk spent walking or driving the dirt roads and trails of your turkey country and listening carefully every few hundred yards will tell you if any gobblers are around. The sound is loud and unmistakable, and to get a better fix on it you can answer the real gobble with one from your box, or hoot like an owl, caw like a crow, bark like a dog, even slam your truck door—I've known gobblers to respond to all of those sounds. Be warned, though, that there are times and weathers when male turkeys simply won't gobble, as when a low-pressure system is moving into your area, or later in the season when the birds have already assembled a sizable harem. At times like these it's best to search for sign during the middle part of the day: scratched-up feeding areas or droppings under potential roosting trees.

Over much of their range, wild turkeys like to roost on the lower horizontal limbs of pine trees—white pines in my New England territory—so be sure to mark the clumps of pines from which you think those bedtime gobbles are coming. Next morning, well before first light, you should be in the woods, about fifty or a hundred yards uphill from the suspected roosting tree, clad in camo, your calls at hand, set up with your back against a broad tree trunk and your gun ready to be raised with minimal movement.

As the gray light begins to filter through the woods, the first sounds you'll likely hear are tree-yelps—soft, muffled squeaks that are the turkey's equivalent of the moans, groans, and curses we (or at least I) make on awakening each morning. Then you'll hear sounds like a sheet or blanket being shaken—it's wing-flapping, the morning wake-up stretch—and you can imitate it by slapping your cap against your leg.

Next, the gobbler will start sounding off his territorial imperative. You can often provoke this clarion call with an owl hoot, but don't overdo it—Old Longbeard has heard it all, and he didn't get that big by being dumb. Compared to the earlier noises, his first gobble will sound like a bugle call—right on top of you, if you've marked the roost well. (An older, trophy-sized tom has a clear, melodious gobble. Jakes, like teenagers, tend to have squeaky voices.) Then—sometimes as much as half an hour later—you'll hear the gobbler fly down, a sound I can only liken to that of someone falling down the cellar stairs with a basket of wet wash.

Early in the season, a gobbler won't be interested in breakfast. What he wants is sex. He may already have a harem of hens who've roosted near him, and will begin courting them the moment he hits the ground. This makes it tough for the hunter, because if you start to make seductive hen yelps, cutts, and cackles on your box or diaphragm call, the real hens will do their damnedest to keep that gobbler from straying. I've known hens to run up to me, ready for a fight, where I sat clumsily imitating them, and I've seen others, more often than I care to remember, purposely cut off and distract a gobbler who'd begun responding to my plaintive calls.

Later in the season, and sometimes later in the mornings during the early season, the hens will wander off from the gobbler to feed or sit their nests, but the old patriarch will still be horny. Your chances of deceiving him are better at these times, and sometimes you'll get a gobbler and two or three jakes charging you all at once. One morning a few years back, I was set up on a shoulder of Shatterack Mountain in southwestern Vermont, calling to a gobbler at least a quarter of a mile across the hollow on the slopes of Moffat Mountain to the east. I must have said something right, because he suddenly began sprinting toward me, as fast as a running dog. Down he poured with two jakes hot on his trail, across a dirt road, and up toward where I sat. A little fold in the ground ahead of me obscured him for a minute, but quicker than I could raise my shotgun he was on top of me—not five yards away. As he saw me raise the gun, he turned to split—but I hit him, hard in the neck, and he flopped. The jakes then came skidding to a halt atop the fold. One of them got airborne, right over my head, and I centered him on the rise. . . .

More often than not, though, you'll have to work your birds long and cunningly to lure them within shooting range. There are countless devices on the market for calling turkeys, from hinged-lid cedar boxes to slate-and-peg scratch calls, from one-handed plunger calls to wing-bone suction yelpers to mouth-held diaphragms. The Dunn's catalog alone lists seven full pages of turkey calls. Most of them come with instructional videos that will teach you turkey talk and how best to use the calls. For starters, though, all you really have to master is:

1) *The Cluck*—a short, single syllable, which varies in volume and sharpness depending on what the hen wishes to say (softer for reassurance, sharper for calling her brood to attention).

2) *The Yelp*—a two-syllable sound, the first note higher pitched than the second. They usually occur in an evenly spaced series of two or three yelps.

3) *The Cutt*—a choppy, high-pitched, rapid series of yelps used by the hen to excite a gobbler during the mating season. You can often call back an alarmed or disillusioned young gobbler with an insistent series of cutts.

4) *The Alarm Putt*—a very loud, sharp series of distinct clucks, which sounds, as a friend of mine says, like fingernails on a blackboard. I sometimes use this call, with a mouth-diaphragm so my hands are free for the gun, at the last possible moment to bring a gobbler's head

upright when he's fanned and strutting toward me; then I sight quickly on his neck and shoot.

As you gain skill with your calls, you can play with other turkey sounds, like the Kee-Kee Run (a whistle or whine, three notes rising in pitch, made by young turkeys when they've been separated from their mother during the fall season, which is best imitated with a diaphragm call) or the Purr (a reassuring, musical whirring or fluttering noise, which you can imitate by pursing your lips and making like an outboard motor; it sometimes will bring a reluctant gobbler those last few steps into shooting range).

There are many variations possible within this simple avian language—subtle tones, little billings and cooings, a certain Stradivarius-like range of possibilities from raspy vibratos to silken siren calls, all of which will come to you with practice. And there is no better place to practice them than in the spring turkey woods—whether they're the blooming dogwoods and shadbush of New England, or the blue-flagged palmetto swamps of southern Florida; among the wild crocuses of the Rockies, or the myriad wildflowers of the Texas Hill Country.

There are six subspecies of *Meleagris gallopavo* in North America and a seventh bird of a totally different genus and species, *Agriocharis ocellata,* in Central America. We'll concern ourselves here only with the Meleagrids, all of which talk the same language and behave similarly, with minor variations depending on habitat. All of them have a 270-degree field of vision and can see about eight times more acutely than a human being. Their hearing is much sharper than ours as well. None of them are easy.

Meleagris gallopavo silvestris, the eastern wild turkey, ranges from New England to the Mississippi/Missouri drainage, and down to about Orlando, Florida, and northern Oklahoma. It had the widest original range and is the largest and most adaptable of the subspecies, running up to thirty pounds maximum. (Domesticated strains like the Broad-Breasted Bronze, bred solely for size, have been known to weigh as much as seventy pounds). All wild turkeys are omnivorous, and a Virginia study showed *silvestris* eating as many as 354 species of plants and insects. Still, given its druthers, the eastern bird prefers "hard mast"—acorns, beechnuts, hickory, and butternuts. These birds like to roost on the long horizontal lower branches of white pines. Their tail tips are dark brown, with iridescent brown-tipped rump coverts.

M. g. osceola, the Florida wild turkey, generally weighs less than the eastern but is taller, with longer legs—the better to run through the wet palmetto hammocks it calls home. More streamlined than the bulky easterners, it has a smaller head that sometimes makes it look, at first sight, like a great blue heron. It feeds on grasses and insects among the palmettos, and on scrub oak mast in drier country. Its coloring is the same as the eastern bird. Any turkey you kill south of Disneyworld is most likely *osceola.* Vermont's Bart Jacob, the author of a fine book called *The Grand Spring Hunt,* now sadly out of print, has killed a U.S. Grand Slam—all four subspecies found within American borders. He feels the Osceola is the wiliest of the American turkeys. "They're on their original range," Bart says, "and they've always been hunted hard."

M. g. intermedia, the Rio Grande turkey, is primarily a bird of southern Texas, though it ranges on up into Oklahoma and the northern Texas and northwestern Oklahoma panhandles, where it overlaps with the eastern subspecies and with Merriam's turkey, the Rocky Mountain bird. In my experience, Rio Grande turkeys run in larger flocks than any of the others—I was once almost trampled by a "herd" of at least two hundred of them, while I was stalking an Indian black buck on the YO Ranch in the Texas Hill Country. They range through open grasslands, searching out insects, plant life, and of course the ubiquitous shinnoak acorns. They'll travel up to five miles to roost in trees no taller than a man if nothing better presents itself. They have white tail tips and cinnamon rump coverts.

M. g. merriami, the Merriam's wild turkey, is bigger than the Rio Grande, about the same size as the eastern subspecies. It loves the high country, roosting and ranging up and down the Rockies through ponderosa pine and piñon country, where it makes a living from pine nuts and acorns from Gambel's oaks, along with the other standard incidentals. Unlike the eastern turkey, the Merriam's tends to feed downhill from its roost, so it's best to set up below them once you've located an arboreal dormitory. Here-today-and-gone-tomorrow is the watchword on these birds—they'll migrate as much as forty up-and-down miles in a day or two. You'll have to scout hard to find them, but once you do, they're a bit easier to fool than the more heavily hunted eastern, Florida, or Rio Grande birds. Many western turkey buffs don't even bother with camouflage while hunting them, and they seem to answer even mediocre calling—I ought to know, since that's my forte. Brilliantly bronze-colored, the Merriam's has creamy white tail tips, white rump coverts, light gray-white secondaries, and distinctive white wing patches—a spectacular bird in keeping with its country.

M. g. mexicana, the Gould's turkey of Mexico and the southwestern U.S. border country, hangs out at elevations of forty-five to seventy-five hundred feet, mainly in the Sierra Madre Occidental. Its preferred food is manzanita berries. Because the country it inhabits is steep, arid, hot, and dusty, it's the most physically difficult of the subspecies to hunt. Its coloring is similar to that of the Merriam's.

Meleagris gallopavo sp., the Mexican progenitor of all the world's domestic turkeys, is probably extinct in the wild—or so say the experts. Originally tamed by the Aztecs, the birds were shipped to Spain by Cortez's conquistadors in about 1520, and quickly spread through the rest of Europe, where they were lumped in the folk consciousness with guinea fowl from the Ottoman Empire. As a result, both birds were known as "turkie fowles." When the Pilgrims arrived in Massachussetts in 1621, they brought domestic turkeys with them, not realizing that tastier wild birds would be virtually free for the killing in the New World. Now we know, but it's a lot tougher today.

Though many states, especially in the West and Southwest, allow the use of rifles for turkeys, some modern variant of the old Pilgrim blunderbuss is still the best and most exciting way to hunt the Big Bird. You have to get them in close for the shotgun, and that's what the game is all about. To see a gobbler in full display, chest puffed and glinting as he struts, the great fan spread, and that bald knob changing colors from red to blue to bone-white as rapidly as a neon sign—to hear him spitting and booming sweet nothings to what he thinks of as his prospective mate—and then to lure him even closer, within twenty-five fatal yards at least, is a nerve-corroding experience rarely equaled in any other form of hunting. When you finally hit the trigger, it's almost an anticlimax.

But you'd better lay it on him accurately and hard, right then, with the right gun and the right load, or it all will have gone for naught. A mature turkey is tough; he can absorb a lot of shot and then get up from what you thought was surely a knockout blow and run like a cheetah clear out of sight. The next news you'll have of him is from the crows circling over some far-off glade where he lies dead from your misplaced shot—unless you do things right.

A wild turkey is a big-game animal, and it's just plain criminal to shoot him with anything lighter than a 12-gauge. Sure, you can luck out and kill the odd bird with a 20-gauge, I've even heard of its being done with a .410, but that's show-off stuff. A friend of mine, Tim Joern of Whitefish, Montana, uses a 10-gauge, a hellacious weapon nicknamed "Big Bob," and doesn't feel he's overgunned. Nor do I.

A big-bore, full-choked, short-barreled, matte-finished autoloader is your best choice for a turkey gun. If you're calling well and the birds are hot, more than one turkey will sometimes repond to your allure— a big gobbler and perhaps as many as two or three jakes, all coming on the run. The autoloader allows you as many as five shots—if it's legal in your state to take more than one turkey—and the noise of the action is masked by the explosion. Very few gunners this side of the late Steve McQueen in a movie called *The Getaway* can work a pump action fast enough to hide the corn-shucking clamor of a moving slide. Pumps are all well and good for waterfowl, where the tolling birds are out in the open with nowhere to go but up once you've fired. But turkeys not hit by your first shot can turn on a dime and disappear back into heavy cover the instant they've located the source of that loud ugly noise.

My second choice for a turkey gun, oddly enough, is an over-and-under 12-gauge Beretta, the gun I use with different choke tubes for pheasant, sage hens, ducks, and geese. I screw in extra-full choke tubes, the tightest I've been able to find. The gun has two beads on the rib, which allows a fairly close sight picture. The advantage of the double over a pump is the silence between first and second shots. Ivory hunters in Africa preferred double rifles for that same reason. Rarely can an animal or bird at close range locate the source of your first shot simply by the bang. The sound of a working bolt or pump slide, though, is a dead giveaway. Then they're gone.

The minimum gun sights you should use are the abovementioned twin beads. Most shotgun manufacturers now market specially designed turkey guns, short in the barrel, with sling swivels already attached (a real convenience), and—most importantly—mounted with either reticles like the Accu-Sight, or buckhorn-and-bead. Some of these have the rear of the front blade painted white or blaze orange, and for a reason. A black bead does not show up against the dark outline of a wild turkey. And a gobbler, even when he's totally deluded by your calling and strutting in full display, holds his head down on his vaulted breast. You want to shoot for his tucked-away neck, not over it or below it. Make sure you can see your front sight against a dark background. One way to get a strutting turkey to raise his vulnerable head and neck is to give an alarm putt on your diaphragm or box call at the last moment, when he's within shooting range. Almost inevitably, he'll stretch out to full height if only for an instant. That's when you hit the trigger.

As to loads, I use as much lead and powder as I can fit in—3-inch magnums—packing buffered No. 4 or No. 5 copper-plated shot. Buffered loads are packed with plastic dust, which holds the pattern together the full length of the barrel. The copper plating keeps the shot from deforming in the barrel, and makes for better penetration when it arrives on target. Bart Jacob, who's hunted them all, tells me that before he hung up his shotgun in favor of the bow some eight years ago, he used to shoot two magnum loads of No. 4s up front, backed by a load of No. 2s for a "finishing shot." With that kind of punch, he could kill out to forty yards—though he tried to get the birds within twenty and usually succeeded.

That said, good hunting, but make sure you kill them stone dead. A bird this grand deserves no less.

Turkey hunting can be hazardous. You're wearing camouflage, you're working close to birds in heavy cover, you're making sounds like another turkey, and you're probably shooting magnum 12-gauge loads of heavy shot—usually No. 4s or No. 5s backed up by No. 2s, any of which can kill a man stone dead at close range. Here are some things *not* to do in the turkey woods if you value your hide and those of your fellow hunters:

DON'T wear any clothing that is red, white, or blue. These are the colors of a gobbler's head, their intensities varying with his state of excitement, and it's the head of the turkey that any other hunter will be shooting at. Some hunters, even seasoned veterans, get carried away with self-delusion. Don't let yourself get carried away in a body bag as a result. I saw a story not long ago about a turkey hunter who was answering the call of nature. He had lowered his camo pants and assumed the position when a nearby hunter saw the white flash of his underdrawers. The victim survived, but now answers to the name of "Half-Ass."

DON'T set up in the open. Not only can an approaching gobbler see you more easily out there, but your seated upper body, especially in low light, will look to another hunter about the size, shape, and color of a turkey's. Always set up with a tree trunk or boulder at your back. Don't rely on immobility to spare you: Believe me, you'll twitch or sway or move your arms, if only in working your call, and another gunner may well mistake you for the gobbler of his dreams.

DON'T stalk or shoot at turkey sounds. Most serious turkey hunters these days sound enough like the real thing to fool even the experts. In the crowded East, particularly, any turkeylike sound you hear on opening day, from yelp to cutt to cluck to gobble, will likely be that of another hunter. Even owl hoots are suspect. Shortly after I moved to Vermont in 1979, two hunters just down the road from me stalked each other sonically for nearly an hour. It only ended when one had killed the other.

DON'T gobble, especially in heavily hunted areas like New England or the South. Sure, you can often draw in a horny gobbler by making sounds like a rival. But a gobble might also draw the fire of some trigger-happy neophyte only too happy to take a "brush shot" and see what he's hit later. Out West you might get away with it, but you never know.

DON'T *call while you're on the move.* That's only asking to be bushwhacked. If you hear something authentically turkeylike, set up quickly while covering your back, and only then attempt to establish a dialogue.

DON'T *wave at any hunter until you're sure he recognizes you as a man.* He has probably heard something, possibly you, and thinks the moment is at hand for the triumphant conclusion of his season. If you wave, he might shoot—and it'll be the end of yours. When I see another hunter, I start singing in a loud, clear voice. My tune of choice? "I Can't Get No Satisfaction."

DON'T *try to pick up a wounded turkey.* Those spurs are sharp, those wings can slap you silly. A dying turkey can pound the crap out of you. Instead, step on its neck to immobilize it, then cut its throat. Don't try to shoot its head off while it's pinned: you might blow your foot away.

DON'T *carry your turkey out of the woods by its feet.* The wings will flap, and another hunter might mistake it for a live bird. Instead, bring along a big plastic garbage bag, or better yet a blaze orange hunting vest to wrap it in. Carry the bird by the neck so the wings hang naturally. A few years ago, a kid in a nearby town was leaving the woods at first light carrying his turkey over his back by the feet. Walking through an open field, he saw a party of hunters going in and waved to them. They turned, their eyes widened, and they let fly. They hit him in the face and neck, but he lived. *Caveat venator. . . .*

ABOVE ALL, DON'T *shoot at anything unless you're sure it's a turkey.* Otherwise you might end up the turkey of the day in more ways than one.

If you cook it right, a wild turkey is to a Perdue Butterball as *pâté de foie gras* is to chalk. The breast meat is sweet, nutty, juicy, the essence of wild meat. The legs are a bit tough but so tasty that to discard them should be a crime punishable by a lifetime loss of license. Along with the carcass, they make a thick, dark, meaty turkey soup so tempting that just a whiff of it can revive the dead—namely me, after a hard day of hunting.

A few basic recipes:

ROAST WILD TURKEY

1) Stuff a drawn, plucked bird with pecans and sliced wild apples—the "feral" apples that spring up in my Vermont turkey woods are often more flavorful than the bland, grainy, libelously misnamed Delicious variety you can buy in most stores. (Picking and choosing them is a hunt in itself, but bring your dog and gun because you'll sometimes flush ruffed grouse in the process.)

2) Add the giblets and perhaps some wild leeks or a quartered onion if you so choose. I do.

3) The fatty "breast sponge" that gives the wild turkey his pouter pigeon look should provide adequate self-basting; but if you're in doubt, lay a few flitches of unsalted bacon over the breast for added moisture.

4) Rub butter or oleo onto the legs.

5) Cover the breast, legs, and sides with a roomy tent of aluminum foil to further the moistening process. The bird should baste itself, but if you want to take the time—and enjoy the fragrance more intensely—you can baste it every half hour with melted butter and the juices that drip into the roasting pan.

6) Roast in a 350-degree oven for ten minutes per pound. Turn the oven down to 325 if the bird is getting too brown, i.e., dry.

7) Remove the bacon and the foil tent for the last half hour or forty-five minutes, to allow the bird to brown properly and the skin to get crisp.

8) Serve with salad, wild rice or potatoes, and a gravy made from the drippings. I like a little cold cranberry or wild elderberry jelly as a condiment. A chilled merlot or white zinfandel goes well alongside. Upmanns for dessert—smoke 'em if you got 'em.

HOT TURKEY SANDWICHES

If there are leftovers from your roast turkey, and there will be if it's a trophy bird of twenty pounds plus, save the meat. You've got a lunch or two in the offing—one you'll never find on the menu at Lutêce.

1) Slice the cooled meat of the thighs and breast about a quarter of an inch thick, across the grain.

2) Fry the sliced meat in an already-hot pan, lightly oiled, for a minute or two on each side. (Use your judgment here—you don't want food with the texture of leather.)

3) Heat up the leftover gravy, or make some fresh from the drippings in the pan.

4) Cut a few slices of my wife's home-baked multigrain sourdough bread, or whatever, and toast them if you choose. Butter them lavishly. Pour some gravy over the bread and the turkey. Slice a big, fat dill pickle or two and lay them on the plate. Also some green onions and a hefty dollop of the aforementioned sauce.

5) Pop a beer—the best musical prelude to the feast to follow.

TURKEY SOUP WITH WILD MUSHROOMS

This is the turkey's long good-bye—each bowl of soup a reminder of the hunt, and thus a joy in its own right.

1) Cut up the carcass with game shears, add the legs and wing bones, and dump all of it in a pot.

2) Add cut-up onions, garlic, celery, carrots, a bay leaf, a teaspoon of thyme, six peppercorns, two crushed juniper berries, and some parsley.

3) Cover with water and/or chicken broth.

4) Bring the mixture to a boil, then simmer it until the meat begins to fall from the bones. Add liquid as needed.

5) Peel the meat from the bones and set it aside to cool—you can add it later, but if you cook it too long the meat becomes tasteless, though the soup will be enriched in the process. Return the bones to soup pot for suption.

6) When the soup is thick enough, replace the meat and add dried chantarelles or whatever wild mushrooms you've picked that year.

7) Eat it.

No study of Meleagrid cuisine would be complete, however, without Scott Fitzgerald's recipe, as follows:

TURKEY HASH

"This is the delight of all connoisseurs of the holiday beast, but few understand how really to prepare it. Like a lobster, it must be plunged alive into boiling water, until it becomes bright red or purple or something, and then before the color fades, placed quickly in a washing machine and allowed to stew in its own gore as it is whirled around. Only then is it ready for hash. To hash, take a large sharp tool like a nail-file or, if none is handy, a bayonet will serve the purpose—and then get at it! Bind the remains with dental floss and serve."

Bon appétit!

AN ENDLESS DEBATE

About forty years ago the late, great Corey Ford wrote a story called "You Could Argue All Day." I've been debating it ever since. The piece was one of his "Lower Forty" columns for *Field & Stream* in which the club members—Doc Hall, Angus McNab, Colonel Cobb, Judge Parker, Cousin Sid, and Dexter Smeed—are gathered as usual around the stove in Uncle Perk's general store. They've just finished a hard, wet day of upland gunning, and as they pass the jug and cut slices of rat trap cheese, they begin to discuss the merits and wiliness of the various game birds on which their lives, loves, and blisters are focused.

Uncle Perk, the crusty New England storekeeper, allows as how "they ain't but one favorite bird, and that's the pa'tridge." The erudite Doc Hall disagrees, opting for the woodcock, and launches into a lengthy mathematical lecture on how he computes his lead on a fast-flushing timberdoodle in heavy cover. But Judge Parker breaks in: "And by the time you've got all that figured out . . . your woodcock has disappeared into the next county, and you're apologizing to your bird dog again. If you want real shooting and plenty of it, there's nothing like doves."

Colonel Cobb, of course, pooh-poohs that notion and pronounces the wild turkey the best of all game birds, an assertion that Cousin Sidney counters with a paean to the bobwhite quail. The parsimonious Mr. McNab, of course, is partial to the ringneck pheasant: "Luik at how much more meat ye get for the pr-r-rice of a shell."

When they've all had their say, Dexter Smeed points out that no one has yet produced a single piece of game as evidence of success on this day's hunt. He reaches into his game pocket and pulls out a rabbit—then sprints for the door as someone hurls it after him. . . .

"Favorite" can mean different things to different people, and all comparisons are odious, of course, but few of us can help arguing the main points of the Lower Forty Club's debate in our own terms, particularly as we get older and gain more experience in the infinite number of ways a game bird, of whatever species, can embarrass or delight us. I've probably been fooled more often by ruffed grouse than any other bird, if only because I've hunted them longer. It sometimes occurs to me that if I had just one breast feather from every partridge that has flushed away from me while a tree trunk obscured its flight path, or exploded within range just as I was stepping through a barbed-wire fence, or waited to fly until my gun and I were hung up in a wild grape tangle, I could go into the quilt-and-pillow business, big-time.

As the first upland game bird on this continent to confront firearms, the New England ruffed grouse has had some three centuries to learn its Houdini-like escape routines. Or to put it another way, all of the "fool hens" were eliminated from the gene pool a long, long time ago. By the late nineteenth century, the ruff—at least east of the Alleghenies—was already as wily as he is today. Edwyn Sandys, in his book *Upland Game Birds*, published in 1902, had this to say:

> The habits of the grouse vary somewhat in different localities, but as a general rule it is to be found in what is termed heavy cover, usually another name for the worst there is in that particular section. A snarl of thickets, swamps, dense second growth, brier patches, heavy woods, beech ridges, dark ravines, forested hill and mountain sides, the brushy banks of streams— each and all find favor with the strong, swift fliers, and right well do they know how to make the most of every protective feature of their chosen ground.

Let me add an embarrassing footnote to that statement. According to Sandys and many other authorities, ruffed grouse are *never* found in the open. Yeah, right. One afternoon, toward the end of a long and fruitless day afield, I was pondering this truism as I trudged across a field toward a final grouse covert. I'd already missed three or four birds in heavy cover, and was wishing that once, just once, a ruff would get up like a gentleman, with nothing around him but air, giving me a clean, open, going-away shot. Sure enough, a moment later—*VAR-O-O-O-O-M!*—a lone grouse flushed from nearly beneath my feet and made a beeline for an overgrown stone wall some two hundred yards away. He was flying straight, no higher than my eyeballs. It seemed I could see his every feather cleanly etched in the late-afternoon light, the unbroken bar rimming his long, gray fan like a funereal band of black velvet. Just what I'd prayed for. I raised the gun . . . and missed him twice.

Woodcock, too, can make fools of us, all the more easily because they hold so tight before they flush and seem to fly so weakly compared to grouse. I wonder if the piping twitter of their wings doesn't signal something soft to our hearts, while at the same time breeding unwarranted confidence in the shooter. Unlike the roar of a grouse's flush, or the rattle of a cock pheasant going off, the woodcock's whistle sounds plaintive, almost pleading. We—or at least I—may unconsciously respond by leavening the shot charge with pity, pulling off slightly to the right or left, up or down, and thus missing the bird. A wing-tipped woodcock sometimes will stand boldly facing the dog or man that comes to retrieve it, fanning its tiny tail like a strutting tom turkey. I used to see this as a gesture of defiance, courage in the face of certain death, but I recently read in a *Stokes Nature Guide to Bird Behavior* that the woodcock fans its tail simply because it's frightened.

More often than not, my mistakes on woodcock come from shooting too fast when the bird rises. You usually find them only in the densest of cover, in the poorest of light, and you know that once they reach the height of their initial jump, they'll take off zigzagging through the upper twigs of the covert, as easy to hit as a frightened bat. Walking into an alder thicket or a stand of whippy young aspen, knowing that woodcock are likely to flush, my heart rate escalates and my nerves are stretched taut. As a result I sometimes shoot when the 'cock is still too close. I was hunting a vast alder brake in New Brunswick a few years back with the writers Charles Gaines and P. J. O'Rourke, having a wonderful morning of it, when my black Lab Luke jumped about the twentieth 'doodle of the day. I was so hyped that I shot too soon and scattered blood and feathers all over my Micmac Indian guide, Gilbert Sewell. Gilbert yelped and I uttered a loud, doleful curse. Charles, who wasn't twenty yards from us but couldn't see what had happened, thought for sure I'd shot Gilbert. "Nah," P. J. said, coming up to survey the damage, "he only splattered another bird." I'll never live it down.

I'd agree with Ford's Judge Parker that the mourning dove is "just about the fastest thing that flies. You aim at the first one coming past you, and if you lead it enough, you'll maybe hit the last one in the line." Nothing can breed humility in the breast of even the most cocksure wingshooter than a hot, fast day in the dove field. It's easy to go through a case of No. 8 shells just filling a twelve-bird limit. Doves are not only fast, they're capable of aerobatic manuevers that would put even a Focke-Wulf pilot to shame. But if you think the mourning dove is swift and dodgy, you should see his big brother, the whitewing.

I've shot them in Baja California, as the guest of Bud Parr at the grand old Hotel Cabo San Lucas, shooting them over the water holes where they come in at dawn to wet their whistles, birds pouring in from every direction, twisting black blurs against the sunrise red sky, shooting until my shoulder ached, seeing some fall but most fly off unscathed, and I've come away from those encounters with a brain full of tangled vectors that took weeks to clear. Talk about computer overload.

Bud owned a pair of matched, specially tooled Parkers, valued (he said) at $125,000 apiece, and late one morning in the cactus thickets he allowed me to shoot one of them. I'd never shot a double gun worth more than 1 percent of the Parker's value, but it certainly lived up to its reputation. The birds were thinning out by that hour—about 9 A.M.—so I stood for a while, hefting the gun and admiring its engraving. "*¡Hola, palomas!*" yelled one of our Mexican "retrievers," pointing about fifty yards away where a pair of whitewings came whipping in low over the tops of the pitahayas.

"Take 'em," Bud said.

"Too far," I said.

"*Take 'em!*" Bud said.

I upped and swung and hit the trigger just as the flight paths of the two doves intersected. By God if they both didn't fall.

As the Mexican ran out to retrieve, I handed the gun back to Bud.

"No, kill a couple more," he said, grinning at me as proudly as if he himself had made the shot.

"Thanks, but no thanks," I said. "I'll stay with two for one, and never forget it."

That was twenty years ago, and I haven't.

Though wild turkeys are certainly exciting, I can't go along with Colonel Cobb's contention that they're the best or even the most difficult of game birds, for the simple reason that we don't usually shoot them on the wing. "Most challenging" I'll give him, though, at least from personal experience—my success in calling trophy-sized spring gobblers into range is virtually nil. But turkeys aren't all that difficult to hit when they're flushed into flight. By comparison, from a standing start a turkey is to a quail as an eighteen-wheeler to a fuel dragster.

Late one afternoon my dog and I were returning from a local covert called Bass Hill after a good day on grouse when Luke suddenly got birdy. But he also got puzzled. I could see he'd picked up a strong scent. He stuck his nose in the air to catch the light breeze, then put it down to the ground in a search for foot spoor. Finally he looked up—the only direction left. With that a flock of turkeys took wing from the maple branch where they'd been roosting, immediately over our heads—a family group, maybe a dozen nearly full-grown poults and a larger hen. I shouldn't really say they flushed—*lurched* was more like it, falling a good two or three feet before they gained enough flight speed to climb away from their launch pad. In full flight a turkey is plenty fast, though these were easy targets as they got airborne—fat, slow, and happy. Still, I wondered if my light loads of No. 7 $^1/_2$ grouse shot would penetrate those thick, hard-finished feathers. Doubting it, I picked a young bird, centered it, then swung the gun muzzles a touch to the left and fired, breaking a wing. The turkey fell, spinning, and Luke was after it—a high-speed chase that fully convinced me of the wild turkey's legendary foot speed. Luke finally caught the bird in the meadow far below.

Though I must say, and my wife would agree, that the young, tender bird certainly made superb table fare, I didn't feel very good about my single taste of shooting turkeys flying—it had been too calculated, breaking that wing on purpose. Still, if someone ever arranges a European-style driven shoot on adult wild turkeys, pass-shooting them in full flight at maximum altitude, I'd love to be one of the guns. I'd use a 10-gauge magnum with loads of copper-plated No. 4s.

Having lived and hunted most of my life on the northern limits of the bobwhite's range, I haven't had enough experience on big coveys of the birds to contest Cousin Sid's argument. Most of the bobwhites I've shot have been pen-raised releases, no comparison with the real thing. But I *have* hunted wild California valley quail, in both the Mother Lode country and the Baja, and found them fast, sporty, and succulent—well worth the hours of dry, hot, cactus-spiked walking it takes to shoot a limit.

Back in the mid-1980s I visited the Kenedy Ranch in southern Texas, mainly to hunt deer and an exotic Indian antelope called the nilgai, but managed while I was there to squeeze in a morning of bobwhite hunting in some of the meanest country I've ever walked. It was all Spanish bayonet, prickly pear, and jungly hammocks, wrapped in a thermal blanket of windless, humid, 90-degree air that leached me dry before the sweat could bead on my forehead. The dogs—small, quick, well-trained English pointers—wore rubber booties to protect their feet, but even at that managed to pick up an occasional thorn. We drove from covert to covert in a big pickup, the hunters deployed in jump seats on a metal shooting deck mounted in front of the hood. When the dogs locked on point, off we'd hop, struggle a short distance into the covert, squint against the sunlight, sweat out a pint of precious bodily fluids apiece, and wait for all hell to break loose. The shooting was over in a moment—sometimes at coveys of up to thirty bobwhites that buzzed out of the thorns almost simultaneously in a starshell pattern. I managed to scratch down a couple or three doubles that morning, but most of the birds I killed were singles. The speed of these quail usually put the survivors out of range before I could swing to a second bird. It's easy to see how this kind of shooting could become addictive, and anyone who can double consistently on wild bobwhites has my deepest respect.

I've written at length about pheasants elsewhere in this book, so I won't chew my cabbage twice—except to agree with Angus McNab that few birds are meatier or tastier than a big cock ringneck, especially when stuffed with wild apples and, yes, red cabbage. Of all the upland birds we shoot on the wing, none offers as big and slow a target as a pheasant, though they do take plenty of killing, so your shot must be accurate. As for Dexter Smeed's bunny, I haven't shot a rabbit in twenty years, not because I find them too easy to hit (they aren't) or because I don't like to eat them (they're delicious), but because I don't want my dogs chasing four-legged game. Let your dog chase rabbits and he'll soon be chasing deer. Shots at bunnies are inevitably low, and no matter how well you think you've trained him, your dog might forget his lessons in the heat of the moment and go haring after that enticing white scut, ending up in the path of your shot pattern.

My personal ranking of "favorite" game birds thus runs as follows: 1) ruffed grouse, 2) woodcock, 3) quail, 4) dove, 5) pheasant, 6) turkey. I rate them almost entirely by degree of difficulty—both in the finding and in the shooting. Though a woodcock is arguably easier to hit than a quail or a dove in full flight, I rank it more highly because I love the bird more dearly, and because slogging through a woodcock covert is far tougher than sitting in a dove blind or walking a quail plantation. Difficulty must be the most important element of the calculation if we're not to end up viewing game birds as mere targets.

But in the end, I guess, my conclusions are the same as Uncle Perk's: "You can argue all day, but it ain't whether you hit a bird that matters. It's the fun you have even if you don't."

FOOL'S PARADISE

To my mind, the sportiest game bird in the world is *Bonasa umbellus*, the North American ruffed grouse. Certainly no duck, not even a green-winged teal, can touch it for speed out of the starting blocks, nor any waterfowl for taste on the table, though here you may disagree. Yet to my admittedly prejudiced taste buds even the celery-fed canvasbacks of yore couldn't come close to roasted ruffed grouse, especially when stuffed with wild apples, pecans, and a few slivers of jalapeño. Nor is any dove or woodcock as hard to hit as a sidehill New England pa'tridge, nor any quail as wily—neither mountain nor valley, Harlequin nor Gambel's, button nor bobwhite. And certainly no gaudy cock pheasant for all his long-tailed Oriental splendor can compare, feather for feather, with this modest upland drummer when it comes to sheer, understated elegance—much less present an equal challenge on the wing.

But there are grouse, and there are grouse.

The distinction between the two kinds came clear to me on a trip to Montana's remote Yaak Valley, hard by the Idaho and Canadian borders. John Holt and I had gone there to hunt ruffed grouse with Tim Linehan, whom I'd met when he lived in New Hampshire seven or eight years earlier. Tim was a guide now, for trout on the Yaak and Kootenai Rivers during the summer, and for ruffs and white-tailed deer during the fall. Holt, an outdoor writer, had hunted with Tim the year before. Linehan is a fine fellow, fit and eager and well read, full of an enthusiasm and a lust for life in its best manifestations—which include an equally marvelous and much-better-looking wife named Joanne, and as biddable, smart, and bird-wise a golden retriever as you're ever likely to hunt behind—a wide-ranging, short-flushing gal named Maddy.

Another reason for hunting the Yaak was the presence of Rick Bass, a writer I'd met in Vermont during one of his book tours a year or so earlier. A gentle, thoughtful man, Bass is the author of some of the finest essay, short-story, and novella collections I've read in quite a while (among them *The Watch, In the Loyal Mountains, Oil Notes, The Deer Pasture, Winter, The Nine-Mile Wolves,* and *Platte River*). Rick's roots are in Texas, and he was heading down that way shortly after our hunt to pick up his German shorthair pointer, a young dog named Colter, from a lengthy session at Bird Dog U.

"Colter's about as birdy as they come," Rick said when we rendezvoused with him at his log home in the Yaak, "but he has a strange habit of screaming when he's on point—I mean *screaming*. It sounds like a woman being murdered. At first I thought he had a sore foot or some other injury, but no. He just *screams* with excitement. Maybe he's too keen, but it's bloodcurdling whatever the reason. I'm hoping that some time with a trainer—maybe the exposure to a whole lot of birds—will cure him of it."

We piled into the trucks and headed out hunting. Tim and Rick have located some twenty-five or thirty grouse coverts in the fifty-five-mile-long Yaak Valley. "I'm sure there are a lot more than that," Tim said as we drove along the beautiful tannin-brown Yaak River and wound our way into the hills. "The coverts we hunt are fairly close to home, and after hitting one we rest it for a few days to let the birds forget. We've been getting 2.8 shots per hour this season so far—about one every twenty minutes—and though the state game managers say the grouse population is at a peak right now, I don't believe it. I think it's got a way to go, and next season should be better than this one."

Leaving the trucks beside a dirt road, we dropped over a steep bank with Maddy about twenty yards ahead of us. And as if to underscore the truth of Tim's contention, she flushed a grouse before we could load our guns.

"Stay close, Maddy, *atta* girl, good girl, come on in now, that's *too* far, okay, that's right, *now* you're a *good* girl, Maddy. . . ." Tim talks to her constantly, whistling her in when she ranges too far in her enthusiasm, never chastising, letting her know by his voice where he is, and praising her lavishly for every good move. He reminded me of a chatterbox infielder talking it up with his teammates in the middle of a hot race for the pennant—Whistling Danny Murtagh, say, the "Pepper Man" who played second with the Braves when they were in Milwaukee, where I grew up.

But ten steps deeper into the covert—thick, still leafy, with visibility limited to say the least, i.e., typical early-season ruffed grouse habitat—another bird got up wild with that heart-stopping roar. I caught just a glimpse of a flurrying wingtip but could't mount my 12-gauge Beretta in time for a shot. Still, two flushes in only five minutes . . . If it kept up this way, the Yaak would indeed be ruffed grouse paradise.

It didn't. We hunted hard, across a densely grown sidehill littered with the mammoth, weathered stumps and tops of logged-off ponderosa pine, then pushed down to a marsh-pocked bottomland choked with willow and alder, and the shootable flush rate dropped to about one every twenty minutes. Just like the man said. . . . I fired both barrels at one bird, a swerving, angling, steep-climbing, right-to-left flush, and thought I might have connected as the ruff disappeared into heavy foliage. But I heard no gratifying thump, and Maddy's nose said, "Sorry."

Down near the alders, Maddy got birdy again and jumped another grouse. Rick, who was slightly behind me to my right but carried no gun today (he was toting a camcorder instead), said the grouse had only flown a short distance, probably hopping up into a stand of lodgepoles just ahead of us.

"That's okay," Tim said. "I'll throw a stick and flush him out for you. Once we find him, that is."

It was Maddy who found the bird, stopping almost on point, quivering, and peering upward into the dark needles. This was a full-grown grouse, not a bird-of-the-year. Usually, in the East, only young ruffs play this naive game—and I'm sad to say some hunters I've gunned with have been known to sluice them off their perches. But before Tim could throw to flush it, this bird flew. I swung and dropped it. Maddy ran in for the retrieve. It was a gray-phase bird; the short tailfeathers and broken black bar in the center of the fan-tip proclaimed it a mature hen.

"Good flush, good Tim, good Maddy!" Rick yelled. Then, quite politely, he added: "Good Bob!"

We hunted our way back to the road, jumping deer along the way, then drove to another covert. Already the sun was sloping down over the Selkirks to the west, and we pushed into a thick stand of willows, alders, and lodgepoles that flanked a dry coulee. There were birds galore in here, but most of them—flushing in some cases from five yards out—were impossible to see. I missed another shot, as did Holt. We'd kicked up trouble enough that day, most of it redounding to our discredit.

On the way back to Tim's house, we stopped in the tiny town of Yaak for a beer. Well, actually, two beers. There are twin watering places in town, on opposite sides of the road, one called The Hellroarin' Saloon and the other The Dirty Shame, and Tim wisely shares his clients' thirsty largesse between them. Properly refreshed, we all retired to Tim's snug cabin, where Joanne prepared us a sumptuous feast of roast venison (the Yaak is home to some of the biggest and tastiest whitetails I've ever seen or eaten).

Next day after a hasty breakfast we were back in the grouse coverts. The first one we hit drew a total blank, though it was the grousiest habitat I'd seen so far. But that only illustrates one of the great solemn truths about upland bird hunting: Some days they're there, some days they ain't.

Pushing into another covert, a grouse flushed out of some low, tangled slashings and, like the ruff of yesterday, hopped up into a tree. It was a cock bird, long-tailed and heavy-bodied. I stood in clear sight not ten yards away while Tim readied a throw to flush him. "I know just what he's going to do," I yelled over to him. "See that thick stuff to the left of the tree? He'll break left with the first jump, then line out with the tree trunk between him and the gun barrel."

And he did. I shot, but only knocked down pine branches.

I think that even naive grouse, like this guy, instinctually hate the sight of man—especially a man's eyes on them—so intensely that they want to eliminate the odious image as quickly as possible. It's like a scaredy-cat covering his eyes at a horror show. That's why grouse so often flush out behind us, or with a tree in the way of the shot—so they don't see us any longer than they have to. It isn't smarts so much as an aesthetic consideration.

At midday we stopped to fish a beaver pond high above town for fat, brightly colored brook trout, alas to no avail, then headed for another bird covert. This proved to be the most productive of them all. In an hour's walk we flushed sixteen grouse and took eight shots, but bagged only one bird. I made the shot, left to right, missing on the first barrel but then steadying myself and swinging through with the second. It was a chocolate-hued male grouse, a rare color anywhere and especially in the Yaak where most of the ruffs are of the gray phase. This fellow was rich as a Dove Bar. Since the fan was undamaged by either the shot or Maddy's careful retrieve, I later removed it intact for posterity, dipping the "pope's nose" in borax and pinning the spread tailfeathers on a piece of cardboard. To my eye, such a spread is more valuable than a royal flush. When the borax had dried the moist flesh of the tail base, I'd spray it with insect repellent and mount the fan on the wall of my den, along with those of a few other memorable birds.

We hunted a couple of other coverts as our last day in the Yaak drew to a close. No success. Then, as we came back out to the truck, we saw Joanne's car approaching. She pulled over to ask us how the day had gone and what we wanted for supper, and she agreed to meet us at The Dirty Shame for a quick preprandial libation, then drove ahead toward town. Half a mile down the road, we saw her brake, then heard the honk of her horn. She was pointing to the right-hand edge of the dirt road.

"She probably sees a bird dusting," Tim said.

As Joanne drove on and we pulled up to a halt, we saw it—a plump, dark, mottled grouse of a sort I hadn't seen since my childhood in Wisconsin half a century ago.

"Spruce grouse," Tim said. "You want him?"

I looked at the bird, standing about a hundred yards ahead of us. My father had hunted spruce grouse before I was born, but they were in short supply when I started to hunt and the state had wisely closed the season on them.

"They're fool hens," I said. "Too easy compared to ruffs or sharptails or sage grouse. But let's see how close I can get to him before he flushes."

I got out of the truck, loaded my gun, and started walking purposefully toward the spruce grouse. He kept picking at grit by the roadside, oblivious to his fate. Seventy-five yards, fifty, twenty-five—he was still there, blissfully unaware of danger. He didn't look up until I stood right over him. His eyes were not exactly fearless, but rather so naive and trusting that my heart went out to him.

I looked back to Tim and John, standing beside the truck.

"I can't shoot him," I said.

"See if you can touch him with the gun barrel," Tim said.

I reached out slowly and laid the muzzle against his breast.

With that, the bird spun and flushed so fast I couldn't have raised the gun if I'd wanted to. He lined out strong and hard with that orchestral drumroll peculiar to the grouse family, angling toward a jungly creek bottom, and when he was thirty yards out—I could stand it no longer.

I raised the gun and killed him.

"Sorry," I said to Tim a moment later. "I guess I changed my mind."

The apology was sincere.

Bird hunting will do that to you sometimes, but I still don't feel good about it.

LESSONS FROM A BIRD FEEDER

At our house we always keep at least two bird feeders filled, winter and summer, and often spend hours watching our visitors. After all, the open season on game birds lasts only three months up here in Vermont —four if you count spring gobblers. That leaves eight empty ones to fill. Oh sure, you can polish your boots, mend your brush pants, repaint your decoys, clean your guns or even shop for new ones, and shoot clay pigeons till the cows come home, but none of these time-killing stratagems really adds much to bird hunting knowledge. I've come to feel that every hunter can profit from bird-watching. After all, it stands to reason that the more we learn about individual birds and their behavior, regardless of species, the better we'll understand *all* birds, including those we seek for the gamebag. I've learned some valuable lessons from my feeders, though perhaps they're more aesthetic than practical.

During a long, hard winter some years ago, for instance, a flock of wild turkeys came regularly to dine on cracked corn spilled from the tubular feeder that hangs from a white pine just outside my front window. Soon I began spreading corn for them in greater abundance, sometimes a fifty-pound sack of it every week. A dozen of the big birds trekked in from the deep woods twice a day, morning and evening, until spring. I was surprised to see their usually bald heads feathered in black clear to the tops. Against the snow they loomed like monstrous, melanistic grouse. The acuteness of their eyesight and hearing was uncanny. The sudden pop of a burning log in the wood stove, the creak of a floorboard inside the house—even though muffled by a storm window and another plate of glass—would bring their heads up instantly, as would any sudden movement, even in the half-dark of twilight.

Thanks to my feeders, I've more than once seen a merlin—or "pigeon hawk" in the vernacular—stoop out of a cold, clear-blue winter sky to kill a mourning dove in a great puff of feathers just three feet from me, one of twenty or thirty doves that winter each year at my place, defying the Vermont snow and ice thanks to our handouts. Though ruffed grouse won't come readily to the feeders, I see them often in the mature aspens and wild apple trees that grow nearby, snapping buds and catkins in the dusk of a February evening—loud as teenagers popping bubblegum. It's occurred to me that perhaps if I laid hot-water pipes under the soil along the brook behind the house, I could keep earthworms active all winter and hold at least a small number of woodcock on the premises. Ah, no, forget it—just the pipe dreams of a nostalgic bird hunter in the gloomy depths of winter. . . .

It may sound silly, but even observing the behavior of songbirds around a busy midwinter feeder—whether they be chickadees or nuthatches, juncos or sparrows or jays—has given me valuable insights into the way birds flush, land, perch, walk, run, hop, freeze into immobility, and assert dominance over one another: facets of avian life that I've found translatable into wonder if not practicality afield.

Even so small and shy a creature as the hummingbird can teach us a thing or two. The fact is, hummingbirds were once a major target for nineteenth-century market gunners, who shot them for their skins. (Perhaps that's why they're now so wary in the vicinity of humans.) Carefully preserved in full feather, the skins sold on the London market for as much as two hundred shillings apiece—ten English pounds, or fifty American dollars, a tidy sum in those days. One seaport in Brazil shipped three thousand hummingbird skins in a single consignment, all of them of the ruby-topaz species. Records show that in 1888, twelve thousand hummingbird skins were offered at an auction in London, just a fraction of the four hundred thousand bird skins from North and South America sold there that year.

The jewel-bright, iridescent feathers of the hummer were especially prized by fashion designers for creating elegant feminine accessories—fans, bonnets, purses, capes. Market gunners, mainly in Central and South America, shot hummers on the wing, using No. 10 or No. 11 shot so as not to ruin the delicate plumage. That's some wingshooting. The ruby-throated hummingbird—the only North American hummer that breeds east of the Mississippi—winters as far south as Panama, and would have been fair game for the market hunters. A ruby-throat weighs barely $1/_{10}$ ounce, measures only $3^3/_4$ inches in length, yet has been clocked at speeds of up to 56 mph. What's more, it can hover like a helicopter, dive like a bullet, or even fly backward if it chooses. Amazonian Indians, shooting miniscule clay pellets from their blowguns, were even more successful than shotgunners at bagging the elusive birds.

According to a wonderful book entitled *Hummingbirds: Their Life and Behavior*, by Esther Quesada Tyrell and Robert A. Tyrell (Crown, 1985), the family Trochilidae comprises 116 genera and 338 species of hummers, all of them found only in the Western Hemisphere. They range in size from the Cuban "bee" hummingbird, *Calypte helena*, which measures a scant $2^1/_4$ inches long (the smallest of all the world's birds), to the giant hummingbird of the Andes, *Patagona gigas*, which measures $8\,^1/_2$ inches. Only six of these species breed in the United States, two of them as far north as Alaska.

Small hummers like the ruby-throat, with which I'm most familiar, have the highest metabolisms and fastest wingbeats of all birds. Their blurred, buzzing wings flap from thirty-eight to seventy-eight times a second in normal flight, up to two hundred beats per second in a nuptial powerdive. By contrast, a crow in full flight flaps his wings 3.6 times a second, a vulture only once. A hummer's heart—the largest of any living creature in proportion to its body size—pumps five hundred times a minute even at rest, and up to twelve hundred when the bird is excited. Which is most of the time. And talk about hot—the body temperature of a hummer ranges from 104 to 110 degrees F during the day, when the bird is up and flying, yet plummets to 70 degrees during the night.

All of this takes fuel. A hummer eats half its weight each day, mainly in the form of nectar from flowers (they prefer the red ones) supplemented by occasional insects, either caught on the wing or absorbed inadvertently from the nectar of the blooms in which the bugs have drowned. My wife and I fill our hummingbird feeders with a mixture of one part sugar to five of water. Mixtures as dilute as eight to one will not attract the birds. Fortunately the hummer utilizes nearly 100 percent of the food value of everything it ingests (by capillary action) through its long tubular tongue. Whether it's probing a hummingbird feeder or a daylily blossom, that pale, snakelike organ can flicker in and out and up and down at a rate of thirteen times a second—how'd you like to be kissed by one? Coincidentally, the Brazilian Portuguese for hummingbird is *beija flor*—"flower kisser."

Here's another intriguing thought: A man with the metabolic rate of a hummingbird would run a normal body temperature of 750 degrees F, but to maintain it would have to eat twice his weight each day— 155,000 calories' worth—mainly in sugar-rich Cokes, I presume, with an occasional steak or lobster for protein balance.

Perhaps as a result of this nonstop sugar high, the hummingbird is an aggressive customer. Males and females get together only briefly each spring to mate, then for the rest of the year fight bill and claw whenever they see one another. The smaller, more colorful males usually win. The drab females are less feisty, though in defending their nests (tiny, thimblelike constructions of bud scales, dandelion fluff, and lichens held together by cobwebs or spider silk—the pure white eggs, usually two of them, are no larger than peas) or their own feeding territories, they've been known to drive off much larger birds—titmice, goldfinches, and even blue jays—with the ferocity and agility of their attacks. I've been spooked myself when I was working in the yard and a hummer suddenly buzzed me. It's a loud, scary noise, and you wouldn't like to meet up with a hummingbird the size of a turkey. It might skewer you like D'Artagnan would one of the Cardinal's men. Hummers love anything red. Often they'll zoom up to women wearing lipstick or nail polish, hovering close and loud and sometimes scaring the ladies silly.

Last summer we had at least four ruby-throats using the sugar-water feeders that hang on either side of our kitchen window. During daylight they visited the feeders every four or five minutes. The boldest was a perky little male, replete with a brilliant red gorget, forked tail, black head, iridescent green back, and protuberant, beady black eyes. The other three wore female plumage—gray shading to green on the back, with white throats and longer, more rounded tails than the male. Two of them were probably juveniles. They were much more timid at the feeders than the male, sneaking up to them from below while the male brashly flies straight in. Paper-wasps and honeybees are also attracted by the sweet syrup in the feeders, and when the female-marked hummers show up to hover nearby, preparatory to sipping, the wasps and bees dart up and fly at them. The female and juvenile hummers quickly back off. The male, on the other hand, thrusts at the insects with his rapierlike bill and scares them away. The other day I saw him snap a bee in half and swallow it, then wash it down with a long draught of syrup.

One summer afternoon not long ago I heard a loud, angry buzzing noise and tracked it to the solar greenhouse that flanks our dining room. One of our three cats must have left the screen door open and a hummer had wandered in—a female or perhaps a juvenile from its plumage. It was batting like a luna moth against the plate-glass windows of the greenhouse, trying frantically to get out. When it saw me, it flared its tail and squeaked like a mouse. I finally managed to herd it back out the door, touching it a few times with the palm of my shooing hand. It was hot and soft and I'd swear I could feel its heartbeat pounding like a teeny tiny triphammer.

Back in my early adolescence, when I first read about men hunting hummingbirds for their skins, I was deep in a *Bomba the Jungle Boy* phase (I still have half a dozen of those moldy old yellow-bound novels on my bookshelf). Daydreaming, I'd imagine myself paddling up the inky Orinoco or the cayman-infested Amazon in a dugout canoe, my trusty 12-bore under the thwarts, loaded with No. 10s and wrapped in oily rags against the constant damp, with maybe a blowgun and a supply of both clay pellets and poisoned darts at the ready as well, constantly on the lookout for an anaconda or a jaguar, and I'd lust for the day when I could become a market hunter. But the world has changed, and I know better now, alas, alas. . . .

Market hunting is illegal in this country, though outlaws still poach deer and ducks to sell to fancy restaurants, and others kill bears for their gall bladders or other body parts, and deer for their horns, especially when still in velvet, for sale to the markets of Asia, where such items are esteemed as folk medicines. Instead of hunting for what it will pay me in hard cash, I hunt to fulfill the fantasies of my boyhood, though modern "moralists" would deprive us of even this satisfaction.

MY GIRL FRIDAY

Ive owned pointers and setters in my time, and good dogs they were, but I finally settled on the Labrador retriever as my gundog of choice. For thirty years now they've rewarded my loyalty with fine work and fast shooting on both waterfowl and upland birds, and I thought I'd never stray. I like Labs for their smarts, their steadiness, their calm dispositions, their desire to please, and the fire that blazes from their eyes whenever the game is a-wing. Secretly, though, I've always felt that any dog, regardless of race, creed, gender, or place of national origin, can be taught to hunt birds. All this is by way of explaining why now—in addition to my superb yellow Lab, Kent Hollow Jake—I own the funniest, feistiest little bitch known to dogdom, a terror of a terrier named Rosalind Russell.

I got Roz as a puppy from my pals Joe Judge and Donna Davenport. Joe's a Chessie and Gordon setter man, but for a while he had a combative Jack Russell named Boomer, and acquired a bitch of the breed to provide him with a mate—Mrs. Boomer, known more familiarly as Mrs. B. The trouble was that Boomer always wanted to fight with his canine houseguests. Before Boomer could manage to get himself crunched, Joe dealt him off to a shooting friend, who later reported that Boomer had turned into a superb dove and quail dog. He'd sit steadfast with his new owner in a dove blind, mark down all the kills and cripples, retrieve them on command, and stack them neatly in little piles in the blind. On quail he worked close and flushed the birds as niftily as a springer spaniel—though he sprang even higher when he pounced.

Mrs. B. is no slouch as a hunter herself. Though she weighs only fourteen pounds, she prefers big game to birds. I was talking with Joe on the phone one evening when he interrupted the conversation to give me a blow-by-blow of Mrs. B. stalking an eight-point whitetail buck that was feeding on Joe's front lawn. "She's getting close now, belly down, ears back, he doesn't see her yet. . . . He's looking up, looking behind him. Christ! He whips around and runs for it, she jumps, grabs him by the ass—she's hanging on for dear life! There they go, into the cornfield, the bucktail wagging the dog. . . ."

That doesn't surprise me at all—nothing about Russells does. I had a friend back in the 1970s who had a Jack named Dudley. While visiting him one winter up in the Catskills, we took a walk in the snowy woods with our wives, with Dudley and his littermate, Bentley, frisking ahead of us. We hiked through ankle-deep snow along a frozen creek, the anchor ice light blue beneath the gelid sky, whole cascades frozen in place by winter's bite; and Stephen—an Englishman—said he'd been cataloging the winter with his camera (he was and is a superb photographer). As we turned back toward his home, we passed a house on the porch of which resided two large, black dogs—a Labrador and a Newfoundland. The big dogs came pouring off the porch in a hell of a fury. Dudley and Bentley kept their silence. They raced toward the big dogs with a steadfastness of purpose and such a murderous intent that the Lab and Newfie suddenly changed their minds about home guard duty. They galloped back to the porch. Dudley and Bentley sprang up the steps and backed the big dogs against the front door. The house's owner, a citified gent, then stepped outside and in high color yelled down to us, "Get those hell-hounds out of here or I'll call the police!"

Together the Russells weighed about twenty-eight pounds. The retrievers, two hundred.

Russells were originally bred by a nineteenth-century English parson, the Reverend Jack Russell, who rode fanatically to hounds. His dogs were derived from the fox terrier, and selected for courage, ferocity, speed, small size, and total toughness. They ran with the long-legged foxhounds—often thirty or forty miles a day—and when a fox went to ground, the Russell was sent down the hole to chase it back out. They also were dispatched into badger setts on suicide missions— kill or be killed—and usually emerged victorious, though sometimes lacking an ear or an eye.

In his heartwarming book *Tales of a Rat-Hunting Man*, a tough Welshman named D. Brian Plummer defines the breed thus: ". . . the multitude of canine sins lumped together and called collectively the Jack Russell Terrier . . . whereas as rat killers they were excellent, they rushed in and slew foxes before they could bolt; they were so hard that they refused to give ground to a badger and were thus torn to pieces."

Mona Huxham, in *All About the Jack Russell Terrier*, tells of a representative of the breed named Cindy who fell down a mine shaft. All efforts to save her failed, her yipping grew weaker, and after much soul searching, Cindy's owners decided that, to prevent a slow, agonizing death by starvation, they'd best blow her up with dynamite. "This they did and her cries were heard no more." Soon after the owners got home, though, Cindy showed up at the door—"thinner and dirtier, but at least alive. The explosion had blown up the part where she had been imprisoned. She was able to dig through what was left and although she emerged in a totally different area from the one she had been in before, she found her way home in no time. These little terriers have an uncanny bump of direction."

How could any dog lover help but admire the breed? When Mrs. B. was pregnant with her first litter, I took up Donna's offer of a pup. I didn't really plan to hunt her, but I wanted a bitch in any event, figuring a female would be easier to handle than a male. Yeah, sure....

Roz was eight weeks old when I brought her home from the Chesapeake, and weighed barely three pounds. She fit comfortably in the palm of my hand—so small that I worried, when I first showed her to Jake, he'd think I was offering him a snack. So I kept her in the car while I went in and prepared him for the great event. "I've got a new friend for you, Jake," I told him. "She's very young and very tiny, and you've got to take care of her, be nice to her, show her how to hunt— but don't get any romantic ideas." Just the thought of such progeny was chilling. Jake proved himself a gentleman.

By the time bird season opened, Roz was nearly four months old. She weighed about five or six pounds, her eyes barely cleared the tops of the mushrooms—much less the grass—but she was all heart. Russells are very companionable, indeed they hate to be left behind once they've been bonded, so remembering that Boomer had become a good bird dog, I took her out with us when Jake and I went hunting. What the hell, give it a shot.

At first Roz struggled along underfoot or behind me, yet she never complained. If she caught sight of Jake, quartering ahead of us, she ran to catch up. Even though Jake worked close, she was still too slow, too puppy-clumsy to keep up with the big Lab. But whenever she heard a grouse or woodcock flush, followed by the bang of the shotgun, her ears shot up and she leaped forward—"all atip," as the English say. As the season progressed, she ranged farther out from my footfalls. Late one afternoon, as we were sidehilling our way through some wicked doghair aspen, she was about five yards out from me and inadvertently stepped on a woodcock Jake had blown past. It sprang with a wild twitter from directly beneath her nose, she tried to leap for it, and I popped it at the top of its rise. But Jake got to the bird before Roz could. The light flashed on in her eyes—I've seen it many times, in mutts and in purebreds alike, in every kind of dog: the understanding that *this* is what it's all about, this is *hunting*. From that moment on, it was catch-as-catch-can.

They worked out a clever division of labor. Roz was mistress of the thick stuff. Cover that daunted Jake—and there wasn't much that could do it—was her delight. When she reached full size, weighing a bit more than twelve pounds, she was only ten inches high at the shoulder but twenty-five inches long from her upturned black nose to the tip of her docked, five-inch tail—almost a wiener dog in her proportions, ugly to look at but fun to watch. And fast. She could weasel her way into a tangle of blackberry briers or through the dense, matted blowdowns and undergrowth of the field edges like a tan-and-white flash of ground-lightning, putting out birds that Jake might have missed. I hung a bell on her collar to keep track of her whereabouts in those tangled thorn hells. Whenever she flushed a bird she'd yap angrily at its cowardice. "*Wimp, wimp, wimp!*" she seemed to say. "Why don't you stand your ground and duke it out?"

Then she discovered chipmunks and rabbits. She could dig like a badger, and when I missed the sound of her bell and went looking for her, I often located her from the tall, clattering rooster-tail of dirt her paws threw into the air like a nonstop mortar explosion—only her butt protruding from the hole, tail wagging madly. A Russell's tail provides a convenient handle whereby to pull it from the earth—like extracting a highly animated turnip.

Fortunately a little work with the police whistle eased that problem—two blasts would usually bring her pelting back, running side by side with Jake, but taking eight jumps to his one.

Then came the fateful day. I'd gone down to Joe Judge's place in October for the early duck season, and while I was there got to talking to a couple of other gunners—Jack Barry and Mark Masselink, whom I'd shot with before at Joe's. They mentioned they'd won a Ruffed Grouse Society raffle for a day's shooting at the Tinmouth Hunting Reserve, not far from where I live in Vermont. Did I know the place? Not only did I know it, I'd shot there many times, both the excellent sporting clays course and the stocked pheasants and quail. Tinmouth was first rate. They invited me to share the RGS largesse with them, and I did so gladly.

After a round of clays one frosty Friday morning in late October, we followed a guide named Mike Gallagher and his English setter, Remington, into Tinmouth's vast acreage of woods and overgrown meadows. The ringnecks held tight, as stocked pheasants will, but they proved strong fliers when we kicked them up. After we'd killed perhaps a dozen, Mike took us up to another field, stopping on the way at the clubhouse for a welcome cup of coffee. I'd brought Jake and Roz along with me that morning, keeping them in the Tinmouth kennel while we shot, but now I asked Mike if I could hunt them on our final swing. Sure, he said. Remington had worked hard and could use a break—let's do it.

It proved a mistake. My dogs were manic as hell, having spent the day locked in a kennel with the sound of gunfire echoing all around them—first from the round of sporting clays, then from the pheasant shoot not half a mile distant. They took off into a cornfield like a pair of canine Exocets, putting up half a dozen ringnecks well out of range. I whistled them back and gave them a sulfurous lecture, embarrassing them as much as they'd embarrassed me. They steadied down, and as as we made our way from corn piece to overgrown meadow to woods' edge, Jake began to flush and retrieve birds as he'd been taught. Roz put a couple up, too, which we duly killed and Jake fetched. At the end of the far field, we turned right and began working slightly downhill. The field was studded with young white pines, branched clear down to the ground. My eyes were on Jake, working birdily back and forth ahead of me among some barberry bushes.

"Get ready!" I yelled to Jack and Mark. Jake blew two roosters out of the barberries simultaneously, the others shot, the birds tumbled in streamers of feathers. . . and out of the corner of my eye I saw a white-and-tan object disappearing like a snake into the ground-hugging branches of one of the pines.

Roz was onto a bird—one we'd already walked past, undetected by Jake—stalking it carefully, belly to the ground. Suddenly I saw the bird, a gorgeous cock pheasant, struggling vainly to get airborne, but unable to clear the low pine branches. I grabbed my police whistle to call Roz off—too late. She pounced like a panther. The pheasant was longer than she was, and nearly as heavy. But it was no contest. Her jaws closed on its head. Crunch. . . .

I bulled through the pine branches, grabbed Roz by the scruff of her neck with one hand, the pheasant with the other, and walked back out, up toward the others with my gun tucked under one arm. My face was burning.

"Hey, you got one too!" Jack said, smiling. "I didn't even hear you shoot!"

"You don't want to know about it," I said grimly. I threw Roz's pheasant over to him. "Stick that bird in your game pocket. I'm taking Rozzie back to the kennel."

"Aw, hell, let her hunt on," Jack said, still unaware of what had transpired. "She's calmed down nicely now."

"You don't want to know about it," I said again, heading off toward the kennel. . . .

We finished the afternoon in good order, banging more ringnecks and a few quail as well. I managed to redeem part of the day by making perhaps the longest successful wingshot of my life. A hen pheasant, one of the birds Jake and Roz had flushed wild at the start, got up between me and Jack Barry. I deferred to Barry's shot—he was, after all, the cohost of this expedition—but he didn't take it. When the hen was about forty yards out I swung on her without thinking and folded her with the first barrel. She had flown out over a low cliff, and fell beyond the rim. My Lab had marked her down, though, and went after her at a gallop. He too disappeared over the cliff edge, and my heart jumped into my throat. But I needn't have worried. Jake is as surefooted as a chamois, and by the time I got to the cliff he was already picking his way back up its sheer face, the hen dangling dead in his jolly jaws.

That night we all dined at the Dorset Inn, where Sissy Hicks, one of Vermont's finest chefs, braised some of our birds in white wine and wild mushrooms. I must have gotten Roz's pheasant. There wasn't a shot pellet in it.

Will I ever hunt Roz again?

Cold reason says no, yet I'm such a softie that I probably will. But only on grouse or woodcock, mind you—truly wild birds. Not on pen-raised pheasants, never again. They're not up to her style of hunting.

REVENGE

Thursday, May 6, 1993—5:12 P.M. I'm driving north on Route 315 between Rupert and Dorset, Vermont, in my wife's '87 Jimmy, heading into Manchester to pick her up at the bookstore where she works, then take her out to dinner. Not going all that fast, really; the speed limit here is 45 and I'm under it by 3 or 4 miles an hour. I've brought the dogs along, three-year-old Jake and his tough little Jack Russell sidekick, Roz, who's not yet a year old. Mill Brook parallels the two-lane blacktop, and cow pastures topped by good bird cover slope upward on either side of the road. There's a tricky little juke in the highway right here, a shallow S with a wicked reverse camber to it, where another, smaller brook flows under a narrow bridge.

Just as I enter the bridge over this small brook, the wheel cocked a bit to the right for the entry, a ruffed grouse steps out of the weeds onto my side of the road, about ten or fifteen feet ahead of me. Almost instinctively, I flick the wheel left to avoid the bird, knowing I should-n't do it but at the same time thinking—*Hah, now I know where you live! Come October. . . .*

Beyond the bridge is a farm road. Spring rains have washed gravel and mud down onto the pavement, and as I snap the wheel right again to regain my line, I feel the tires slip on the rubble. The rear end kicks out and the Jimmy is into a left-hand drift. From the corner of my eye, through the flicker of passing telephone poles, I see black-and-white cows drinking placidly from Mill Brook, a golden backlight on the newly leafed aspens, and dead ahead the catch-fence fast approaching. Behind it stands a very sturdy, very immobile utility pole. . . .

Don't ever believe that crashes occur in slow motion—elegant sports cars pirouetting balletically through the summer air at Lime Rock or Spa or the Nürburgring. Car crashes happen faster than you can think.

Whump!

Like that.

Had I died at the moment of impact, I wouldn't have known the difference. No fear, no regrets, no screams, no instant replay of a mis-spent life, no pain, no time even to say, "Aw, shucks!"

Just *Whump-Dead!*

The next thing I know, maybe a minute or two later, the Jimmy's lodged against the utility pole, its gray hood folded back in a shallow V, the steering wheel peeled off its post, the windscreen starred in front of me. Roz Russell is sitting in my lap, licking blood from my chin. I think, *Damn, I'll be late picking up Louise.* I try to crank the starting motor. No go.

Someone's looking in the driver's side window. It's the town's new postmistress, a friendly, pretty, dark-haired woman named Hedie Francis.

"Are you all right?" she asks, wide-eyed.

"Yeah. But I've got to pick up my wife at the bookstore. I'm running a bit late already."

"I'll call for help," she says. She has a queasy look on her face, but Hedie is the soul of efficiency and I know I'm in good hands.

Jake's sitting in the backseat, looking very grave. He doesn't seem to be bleeding anywhere, though. Roz has blood on her but it's mine.

Then Skip Wilson is standing at the window. Somehow it's gotten about ten minutes darker. Skip's the boss of the town road crew, a tall, capable young man, a fine deer hunter, with a black mustache and a squint that makes him look like he's always grinning.

"Dammit, Skip, I can't get the motor to start. You got some jumper cables along? I have to pick my wife up at the bookstore."

"You're not going to any bookstore, Bob," he says. "The Rescue Squad is on the way."

I spent five pleasant days at the Mary McClellan Hospital in Cambridge, New York, most of them in the ICU, with a broken cheekbone; a split nostril; contusions on my chest, neck, scalp, and face; Ubangoid lips; a nose the size of a Russet baking potato; two magnificent shiners—you'd have thought I'd gone fifteen rounds with Mike Tyson; and what the x-rays revealed to be a "bruised heart." I'd also bitten my tongue nearly in half, about two inches back, and that had accounted for a lot of the blood, which must have been welling from my mouth when Hedie the postmistress came up. No wonder she'd looked sick. My chest had hit the steering post. I'd had my seat belt securely fastened and the lap portion of it did its job. But the strap that was supposed to keep my upper body from harm had played out like a tape measure.

Everyone said I should sue General Motors. "Hey, they'll settle out of court, man. You could retire!" But I'd known the seat belt was defective before the crash and had typically procrastinated in getting it fixed. Besides I hate lawyers and lawsuits. And, really, I don't want to retire quite yet. In fact, not ever.

The other thing everyone said was, "You should never, ever swerve for animals—always drive right through 'em."

Even nice little blue-haired ladies told me that.

Even pretty young things who get weepy-eyed over kittens and puppies and baby deer told me that.

And in theory I can see where they're coming from. What's more valuable, they're saying, your life or an animal's? Or more to the point, what's more painful to your pocketbook, an animal's death or the expense of auto repairs—perhaps even the cost a whole new car?

As to the first question, I'm beginning to feel, as I grow older, that the life of one ruffed grouse is worth saving, at least until the opening of bird season. I've never met a ruff I didn't like, especially one that offers me an open, straightaway shot at reasonable range.

As to the second, I'll agree that times are tough right now and costs outrageous. But I can sleep easier at night with an anemic bank balance than I can with memories of wasted game birds. I still have occasional nightmares about a partridge I dropped once, years ago, in heavy cover on a dank, dark, rainy November afternoon before I ever owned a retriever. I knew the bird was dead in there somewhere—I'd centered him in a great puff of breast feathers, his head flopping limply and both wings folded tight to his sides as he tumbled. No way he was walking away from that. I hunted for the bird among the aspen whips and multiflora rosebushes until nightfall, but never found him. Food for the foxes. Now when I dream of him, the dream has that same mucilaginous feel to it as those nightmares where you're late for a final exam you haven't studied for, and you can't remember where the classroom is.

God only knows what they pump into you in an Intensive Care Unit, but while I lay there with a tube up my nose and another dangling from my groin, I had plenty of time to ponder the subtext of the mishap. *This grouse had clearly set out to kill me.* I hadn't known they were that vindictive. But if it was true, I'd surely have to kill him before he got another crack at me.

September 25, 1993—3 P.M. I decided to devote a few hours of the opening day of bird season to a search through the covert from which my Nemesis had emerged. Jake and I followed the brook up a dense, steep little ravine that opened on top into an abandoned pasture. A few gnarled and ancient apple trees studded the field. Tall popples stood at its edge, wriggling their toelike roots out under the blanket of grass. In the old days cows would have cropped the aspen clones that fired skyward from those roots. But now, left alone by man and cattle alike, dense stands of aspen shoots—none thicker than a man's little finger— were slowly invading the field, rising like the hairs on a sleeping dog's neck when something strange snaps outside at night.

According to the late Gordon Gullion, with whom I'd spent a few pleasant, informative days some years ago at the University of Minnesota's Cloquet Forestry Center near Lake Superior, grouse and aspen fit together like tongue and groove. Scatterings of aspen provide good breeding cover for the birds, and thick-sprouting stands of doghair aspen like those in this field afford ideal brood cover for clutches of newly hatched, unfledged grouse. The high stem density of such a thicket makes attacks by low-swooping raptors or pouncing quadrupeds like foxes, coyotes, and house cats much more difficult.

But most importantly, in a hard winter, grouse can fill up on the big, fat flower buds produced by male aspen more quickly and nutritiously than they can on any other food source. "The twigs producing flower buds are stout enough to allow grouse to move around on them and feed with a minimum of wing motion and the accompanying loss of body heat and energy," Gullion wrote in his valuable book *Grouse of the North Shore* (Willow Creek Press, 1984). Grouse will eat more than forty-seven buds a minute, he noted, filling their crops with about three ounces of buds in only fifteen or twenty minutes—"equivalent to a 150-pound person eating 27 pounds of food at one sitting."

This aspen stand where I hoped to settle accounts with my would-be assassin was therefore a grousy amalgam of Alice's Restaurant, the Mustang Ranch, and a top-notch child-care center.

As Jake and I entered the popples, his nose up and sniffing, my 20-gauge Winchester double at high port, I had blood in my eye both figuratively and literally (a few capillaries ruptured in the crash still hadn't quite healed). Jake quickly got birdy, muscles tensed beneath his golden hide, his tail arched tall and flailing as he nosed down into the still-leafy aspen whips for a flush. A woodcock rose on twittering wings and canted sideways like a helicopter as it flashed for heavier cover—but I stayed my trigger finger. Woodcock wouldn't open until October 1.

Pushing on, we reflushed the woodcock, or perhaps another one, and worked deeper into the more mature aspens. It was a hot, sunny afternoon, virtually windless—poor scenting conditions for the dog—and I figured that on such a day the grouse might well be back in the cooler depths of the shade. Back here it was mucky with small seep springs and thick with mature alders, many windfalls crackling underfoot. Tough going. If something got up in this stuff it would be hard to swing the gun. We pushed through the alders into young hardwoods, interspersed with fingerling birch whips, hardhack, thornapples, and blackberry briers, until we hit pole timber, then worked a long, slow zigzag route back toward the field, steering our course from one stunted, heavily laden apple tree to another. Jake checked under each tree for the scent of our prey. Birds had pecked a few fallen, still-green apples, but only halfheartedly so far. They must have had a better food source somewhere else. It was a good nut year—acorns galore beneath the red oaks, and even a few stands of beeches were producing mast. But I had seen none of these in this covert, or in the bigger, more open woods behind it.

By now I was pouring sweat, and Jake's tongue was lolling. He found himself a mucky pool, bellied down in it with a happy grin, and emerged a two-tone Labrador, brown and yellow. We pushed on for half an hour more. The sun was sinking lower now, and, checking my watch, I saw it was a little past 5 P.M. Just about the same time of day that the grouse had nearly killed me. How fitting it would be to kill him at precisely the same minute!

And sure enough, as we neared the edge of the woods, the rich sunset light of the field beyond etching the covert with incandescence, Jake got suddenly birdy. He whipped around in midstride, stuck up his tail, and plunged to my right into a pocket of briers.

Out poured a partridge in a great roaring hurry.

A flying grouse looks twice as long as he really is—head and neck stretched, body attenuated, truncated tailfeathers seeming as long as a pheasant's. I swung with him and through him, eyes locked down the vent-rib on his stubby beak, and just as he broke from the edge of the covert, I hit the trigger. I lost him for a moment in the recoil, but there beyond the gun muzzle bloomed a momentary halo of backlit grouse feathers, falling like jewels against the sunset.

I heard him thump down in the meadow—*Whump-Dead.* . . .

"Fetch him back, Jake."

When he'd brought the bird to hand, I spread the fan—a long one, with an unbroken band of black at the tips of the tailfeathers—a mature cock, not a bird of the year. This could well be the grouse who'd nearly done for me back in May. As I hefted his hot, heavy body in my hand, though, I felt no great sweet surge of vindication, of vengeance fulfilled. I felt only what I always feel when I kill one of these splendid game birds—awe at its speed and beauty, a twinge of sorrow at having ended its life, and a warm glow of satisfaction that we all could have gotten together this way: me, my dog, this bird, and the shot-charge, arriving at the same point at the very same moment.

Revenge had no place in it.

OPERATION FLEABAG

He that lies with the dogs, riseth with fleas.
—George Herbert (1593–1633)

 Old Doc Maxwell's no longer with us, but for many years he was a legend in these parts—a big, longbearded veterinarian, a bon vivant, a superb raconteur, and a stone turkey hunter from the word go. Or perhaps I should say a *stoned* turkey hunter. Doc could be seen in any season, regardless of the weather, pounding the hills and swamps with a 10-gauge Browning in one hand and a two-gallon jug in the other. The jug contained Doc's "universal solvent," an omnipotent elixir of the chase compounded in equal measures of hard cider and grain alcohol. He found it particularly beneficial during the spring gobbler season.

"You know how the blackflies and no-see-ums always start to nip at you in earnest just when you've got a good gobbler working?" he'd say. "Well, if you've steeled yourself beforehand with a few hearty belts of this solvent of mine, your problem's solved. The bites aren't near as distracting. You can have half a million of the noxious little bastards gnawing at your vitals all at once and not even know it. And you won't spook off that gobbler with a lot of last-minute swatting."

Quite early one May morning, Doc was ensconced in comfort against a familiar swamp maple, alternately swigging from his jug and yelping on his hinged-lid Roger Latham "True Tone" squawk box, when out of a nearby thicket came skulking the biggest, fattest boar raccoon he'd ever seen. The brute, Doc determined, was obviously on the prod for a hen-turkey breakfast. What the brute didn't know was that Doc was an omnivore to whom roast raccoon was as delectable as turkey pot pie. In an instant that ringtail was history.

The morning wore on with no further action, and the combined effects of the spring sun, the songs of the migrating warblers, and the babble of a nearby brook, not to mention a few more celebratory draughts of his tasty tonic, put Doc in the mood for a snooze. Dragging the late raccoon over for a pillow, he lay back in the dappled shade, adjusted his bushy red beard over his chest like a bib, and was soon in slumberland. When he awoke a few hours later, the sun was over the yardarm and his beard was hopping with fleas. They had migrated from the cooling body of his erstwhile victim to the warm fuzzy depths of Doc's beard. Not all the elixir in the world could remove them. . . .

Anyone who hangs out with animals long enough will sooner or later encounter what I call The @#$%^&! Flea Problem—perhaps not in so bizarre a fashion as Doc Maxwell, but just as pestiferously. Fleas have been endemic in my household for most of the sixteen years I've lived here. They arrived courtesy of a pair of barn kittens my wife and I acquired to replace a beloved young tomcat named Bone, who'd met his far-roving fate under the wheels of a car on our remote dirt road. We should have taken the kittens to the vet for a flea-dipping session prior to bringing them home, but we'd been so saddened by Bone's demise that we weren't thinking clearly. Before we could get the jump on the fleas, they'd gotten it on my gundogs. Over the years, despite enormous outlays in cash, sweat, and blood—for powders, sprays, foggers, flea collars, soaps, and the application of same to a 3,600-square-foot house plus five animals well armed with claws and teeth to repel our well-meaning ministrations—we've yet to get rid of the invaders. But I've got my fingers crossed.

We recently completed our latest effort at flea control. The summer had proved a particularly favorable one for the proliferation of *Siphonaptera*—humid and cool, yet interspersed with enough hot spells to encourage rampant flea randiness and thus copious breeding. By August the joint was literally jumping with the result—a zillion tiny black devils, each no bigger than a poppyseed, each capable of leaping (if it were human-sized) 546 feet straight up in the air from a standing start, or running the hundred-yard dash in .001 seconds flat through a forest as densely grown as a dog's fur coat. Ah yes, a superb athlete, the flea! And all of them thirsty for blood. In no time, they were driving our cats nutsier than usual, and persecuting even the otherwise imperturbable Jake. Rosalind Russell was particularly vulnerable to their attentions, scratching herself bloody day and night. There was nothing for it. Once again we set the time-honored wheels in motion to eliminate the minuscule millions. Recalling organizational skills from my distant days as a U.S. Navy line officer, I drafted a three-page, four-day, twenty-step order of battle, code-named "Operation Fleabag."

The preparations for F-Day included: clearing and pruning the brush around the house and barn and anointing the area with agricultural pesticides; stacking the burnables in the field behind the house for subsequent incineration; making arrangments for the removal and decontamination of rugs and carpets (estimated at $85); purchasing flea bomb foggers from the local vet (total cost for nine Siphotrol bombs capable of debugging 33,000 cubic feet of house and barn space: $83); taking the dogs' favorite chair to the town dump (they'll miss it but there was no way we'd ever rid it of fleas); clearing off a year's worth of books and magazines from the living-room coffee table preparatory to rolling up the flea-infested rug beneath it; cleaning my office (though I'll never be able to find certain valuble files—ever again, I'm sure); my wife cleaning *her* office (a five-hour task at least—she's no neater than I in that respect); vacuuming the house thoroughly; moving furniture and coffee table off the living room rug (a.k.a. Backache City); rolling up aforementioned rug and dragging all 200 pounds of it out of the house for pickup; covering all eating and food-preparation surfaces with newspapers prior to fogging; removing all exposed chinaware, cutlery, and pots and pans from the house; placing and setting off nine flea bombs in attic, second and first floors, basement, and barn; taking the animals to the vet for dipping ($88.75); waiting two hours for the fog to do its work, while in the interim vacuuming our vehicles and spraying them with flea poison; airing out the house for half an hour; then bringing the animals home—*sans* fleas, we hoped. And at last the final phase of the whole arduous ordeal: taking my long-suffering wife to dinner at the nearby Dorset Inn ($32.75 including tip).

"That's the nicest item of all," she graciously remarked on reviewing the Op Order.

It was all to no avail, though. Next spring the fleas were back. . . .

Years ago I recall seeing some photographs of an eighteenth-century Russian sect called the Dukhobors, who had migrated to Canada to escape religious persecution. Each winter, it seemed, one or another band of Dukhobors would strip themselves naked, leaving their clothing and all of their possessions in their wooden houses, and then set fire to those dwellings. The photos showed the Dukhobors cavorting naked in the snow with their houses ablaze in the background. They seemed quite joyous under the circumstances. The captions explained that they did this periodically to rid themselves of their earthly possessions and all the pride and vanity that went along with them. Oh yeah?

I think they were merely doing it for flea control.

Next time fleas show up in the house, I'll probably join the Dukhobors. Meanwhile I leave you with another little snippet of English verse on the subject of The @#$%^&! Flea, this one by Jonathan Swift:

. . . So, naturalists observe, the flea
Hath smaller fleas that on him prey;
And these have smaller still that bite 'em;
And so proceed ad infinitum.
Thus every poet, in his kind,
Is bit by him that comes behind.

Postscript: There's now a new product on the market that promises total victory in the age-old war between man and flea. It's a drug marketed by the Ciba-Geigy Corporation under the trade name of Program that's sold in tablet form for dogs and in premeasured liquid dosages for cats (who are notorious for their reluctance to take pills). The active ingredient is a drug called lufenuron, a benzoylphenyl-urea compound classified as an insect development inhibitor that breaks the flea's life cycle at the egg stage. The tablets and liquid come in different strengths, depending on the size of your dog or cat. Once a month during the flea season, or perhaps year-round depending on where you live, you simply feed it to your animals—I wrap the pills in a hunk of hamburger, and mix the liquid for my cats into a serving of cheap, stinky canned tuna. They gobble or lap it down quite happily and clamor for more. Then you all sit back and wait. When adult fleas bite your dog or cat, they're unable to produce viable offspring. Program won't kill adult fleas, but eventually they'll die of old age, leaving no next of kin. Voilà! A flea-free home! Still, it takes from one to three months for all of the preexisting fleas to die off. In the interim you can treat your pets with conventional sprays, powders, or shampoos to keep the adult fleas from plaguing them too severely. In our household, as I write this, we're already two months into this latest chemical warfare campaign. Whether we'll win the war or not, I don't know—but I've got my fingers crossed.

IT WOULDN'T BE THE SAME

My friend Edward Hoagland called one day with an intriguing suggestion. Though he's one of the finest nature writers in any language (*The Courage of Turtles, African Calliope, Balancing Acts,* and others), Hoagland doesn't hunt or fish. He'd been asked to review Howell Raines's memoir, *Flyfishing Through the Midlife Crisis,* and wanted to check his understanding of certain angling terms.

Our discussion had gotten around to the subject of catch-and-release.

"A fisherman is basically a predator," Ted said, "and I'm wondering, can a predator's instincts really be satisfied just by hooking a fish and then letting it go?"

"Certainly," I said. "Nowadays I release nearly all the fish I catch. Sometimes I'll spend five or ten minutes reviving them after I've caught them, to make sure they're okay. There's no reason in the world—except ego—to kill, say, a tarpon or a bonefish. They aren't worth eating. Trout are delicious, of course, but they're still more valuable alive than dead. It's more fun to catch them than to eat them, and when you've reduced a trout to a pile of bones, neither you nor any other angler can ever catch it again."

"Wouldn't the same be true in hunting?"

"I suppose so," I said, taken somewhat aback. "But there's no way you could do it."

"Why not?" he persisted. "You could use one of those laser-guns like they have in carnival shooting galleries—you know, the kind that tells you instantly when you've hit the target. You've often said that the climax of the whole bird hunting experience comes at the moment you actually hit the bird when it's in midflight."

Beep—you're dead?

"Trust me," I muttered lamely. "It just wouldn't be the same."

Hoagland later included the notion of electronic bird shooting in his *New York Times* review of the Raines book: "Hunters have not yet had the chance to learn a hunting counterpart to 'catch-and-release,' but I suspect that by the turn of the century some entrepreneur will be earning millions with a radar or heat-seeking technology that tells a hunter when he has 'killed' a bird."

I've been pondering Ted's proposal ever since.

Why *wouldn't* zap-and-release bird hunting be as rewarding as the real thing?

Certainly game birds are at least as valuable, both aesthetically and from a culinary standpoint, as "trophy" trout or even salmon. Some birds—ducks and woodcock in particular—are mighty thin in the air along their flyways of late, as scanty in numbers as trout in many Eastern streams where bait fishermen have equal access with fly fishermen. By the same token, though for different reasons, wild quail are getting harder and harder to find, and a pen-raised bobwhite is to its wild namesake as a hatchery rainbow is to a stream-bred one: pale, puny, and stupid.

So too, for the most part, are the pheasants, chukars, huns, and other pen-bred game birds released by shooting preserves (at outrageous prices) for hunters to bang away at these days.

And for all the talk of "game cycles," most experts admit that the "highs" of each succeeding ruffed grouse cycle produces fewer birds than the previous high—a fact verified by the historical record. Frank Woolner, in his excellent book *Grouse and Grouse Hunting*, talked with an old Massachusetts market gunner of the late 1800s who "told me that 350 birds a man was a fine season's bag." Nowadays even a fanatical grouse hunter—afield every day with a savvy dog and a crack shooting eye—would be hard pressed to kill a quarter that many a season anywhere in New England or the Upper Midwest.

Though studies show that hunters kill only a small percentage of the wild birds that die each year—perhaps 5 or maybe as high as 10 percent—those few birds, if left alive, would undoubtedly breed more birds for the next season. And on and on and on. . . .

Ergo: If no-kill angling can be rationalized by its greater aesthetic value and the ever-lessening numbers of the truly wild fish available to breed, then so too could no-kill bird hunting.

Another consideration is public opinion, which as we all know is swinging ever more stridently against "blood sports" of every kind.

Twenty years ago I was hunting near my home, which was then in the northernmost reaches of New York's Westchester County. The area was still "country" in those days. It was late afternoon and as I neared the two-lane road across from my house, the dog flushed a grouse, which I killed in heavy cover. I went out on the road as the dog made the retrieve, and called him to me. I was just taking the bird from him when a school bus came around the corner and stopped to let off my children. The rest of the kids on the bus just gaped at me through the windows.

My God, what an appalling sight: a man with a smoking gun, his hands all dripping with blood, and a great hairy slavering brute of a dog dropping a dead, harmless little tweety-bird into those murderous meathooks! As the bus drove on past us, the kids pushed up their windows and booed us all.

The boos would be even louder today.

None of the schoolchildren, of course, had ever hunted—none but my own. Those kids didn't realize that the blood on my hands was from brier cuts, they didn't know what it took to knock down a bird in close, heavy cover, nor could they realize the amount of hard work it had taken to make that Labrador retriever a good gundog. They didn't have an inkling of what our hearts felt—mine and the dog's—at the moment when the gun bucked against my shoulder and that bird puffed and tumbled, and the burnt incense of gunpowder wafted back to us. And they never will, no matter how much we talk or write about it. The schools and the newspapers and television and the movies will see to that.

But just as no-kill fishing has altered the public image of the angler—from that of a leering, beer-guzzling, knock-'em-on-the-head trout killer into a gentle, Waltonesque, nature-loving yuppie wearing lots of neat gear—I have no doubt that the sort of zap-and-release bird hunting suggested by my friend Ted Hoagland would at least to some degree alleviate the venomous societal prejudice against us.

Maybe I'm just an old stick-in-the-mud, but I say to hell with it.

The hunt is more than a gallery game. At its best (and at the risk of sounding absurdly uncool) let me say that I feel it can be a sacrament, combining in its ancient sequences—oddly ritualistic but never exactly the same—the basic mysteries of Baptism, Confirmation, Absolution, Transubstantiation, Marriage, and Extreme Unction.

Think about it.

Each time we go afield, we're baptized anew in the fellowship of the natural world. I defy any bird hunter to tell me he doesn't feel blessed by the subtle changes that occur, day by day, almost hour by hour, in even the most familiar of his coverts. Shifting light, falling leaves, winds boxing the compass and changing the angles of a hunter's approach; rain, mud, snow, scorching sunlight—then the always-astounding flush, a fresh revelation each time it occurs, though we've seen it a thousand times before. The bird wings out more swiftly than thought. . . .

Each time we go afield, we're confirmed in our belief that this is where we rightly belong, pounding these hills or wading that swamp, shivering in the cold rustling confines of the blind, pushing through the thorns or pausing to catch our breath on the windswept hilltop, watching the indefatigable dog seek out the truths or falsities of the next thick covert. . . .

Each time we go afield, we're absolved of the petty sins of our daily nonhunting round—of sloth, surely, for we work at the hunt if we're doing it right; of falsity, for there is only truth in the field (the lies may come later, of course, when we talk to our friends about it; but never forget, your dog knows); of greed, if we only shoot them on the wing; of hubris, if we make no excuses for missing; of cruelty, if we shoot straight and kill clean; of lust, if we love and respect the birds we kill; of despair, if we enjoy the bad days along with the good. We pay the penance for our sins in sweat and thorn slashes.

Each time we kill a bird, we die a little ourselves, and in that death renew our love for what we've killed. Each time we kill a bird, we pledge our eternal troth to it, as at a wedding altar. Each time we kill a bird, we anoint it with the oil of our compassion and pray for its soul on the Spirit Road.

And each time we partake of the flesh of the birds we've killed, we become one with their essence.

Hunting is incomplete without death.

That's why it can never be a mere gallery game.

WAMPUM ON WALL STREET

"Of all the grouse family, this bird—the 'chicken' of shooting lore—probably yields the most complete satisfaction to the great army of American sportsmen. . . .Were the cleverest sportsman who ever lived to undertake the designing of a bird of habitat and habits to suit the wishes of perhaps three-fourths of the gunners of this country, the result of his labor would be something very like a prairie hen."

A bird hunting gentleman named Edwyn Sandys penned those words in 1902, when the pinnated grouse, *Tympanuchus cupido*—a.k.a. the greater prairie chicken, prairie cock, prairie grouse, or prairie hen—was still abundant through most of the Mississippi Valley and well into the Great Plains. Sandys went on to cite the bird's "qualifications" for this judgment. It's a big, handsome bird, he said, "vigorous and prolific," strongly barred in black, buff, and chocolate brown, providing nearly two pounds of succulent meat to the table; its grasshopper-eating proclivities make it a friend to the farmer; its ranges can be easily reached by railroad or buggy; it holds tight before pointing dogs; and, most importantly, "it gives the gun a fair, open chance, seldom being found in anything like really difficult cover."

Sandys even went so far as to praise this "big, generous chicken" for offering fair sport to the handicapped: "a one-armed, one-legged, or no-legged man may enjoy his chicken-shooting with the best of them . . . for the chicken may be shot from either the saddle, or any suitable wheeled conveyance, without any need for the gunner to move from his seat. Shooting from the saddle is a method which is common in both West and South, but only the prairie in some form can offer reliable sport to the man on wheels."

Indeed, wealthy sportsmen of the late nineteenth century frequently invaded prairie chicken territory for a month or more at a time, summer and fall, basing themselves comfortably in their own private railroad cars, which would be parked on a siding, replete with manservants, wine cellars, ornate china and silverware, fresh table linen and napery, while the guns fared forth each day in their light spring-wagons, following the dogs and easily killing forty or fifty "chickens" apiece between dawn and sunset.

Sandys saw a glorious future for his favorite sport. "Like the quail," he enthused, "the 'chicken' follows the plough, which accounts for the gradual extension of its range westward, while the narrowing of the eastward limit is readily explained by the increased number of guns and other destructive agencies."

Nearly a century after Sandys wrote his paean to the greater prairie chicken, I had an opportunity to spend a day in pursuit of this wonderbird, on the golden, windswept plains of South Dakota. Alas, the things which Sandys hath seen can now be seen no more—at least not in the abundance he witnessed. For one thing, the prairie cock does *not* follow the plow—in the end he flees from it. Though he did, for a short while at least, follow the lumberman's ax.

The greater prairie chicken once occupied a vast region where the eastern oak forests phased into the tallgrass prairie, making its living before the snow fell from the seeds of big bluestem grass *(Andropogon gerardi)*, sometimes called "Turkey Claw," and from acorns in the winter. The bird's original range encompassed all or parts of what are now Ohio, Michigan, Indiana, Illinois, Wisconsin, Minnesota, Iowa, Missouri, the northwestern corner of Arkansas, eastern Oklahoma, and perhaps half to three-quarters of the vast state of Texas.

There was even an East Coast race of the species, the so-called "heath hen," which thrived in the parklike, fire-spawned "oak prairies" and sandy blueberry "barrens" that occurred from Maryland and north-central Tennessee to southern New Hampshire and Maine. But finally, pressured on all sides by murderous humanity—my own beloved grandfather, a sometime market hunter, among them—the heath hen was reduced to a remnant population on Martha's Vineyard. The last of the race died in 1932. My granddad followed in 1957.

As the vast white pine forests of the Upper Midwest were felled, to be replaced by small farms growing corn, wheat, or millet, the greater prairie chicken—always more abundant than the heath hen—moved north into territories it had never occupied before, like the former North Woods of Wisconsin and Michigan's Upper Peninsula. For a brief while, the birds actually benefited from these new sources of feed, learning to glean among the harvested fields of small grains. As long as enough virgin prairie remained for courtship, nesting, and brooding, they thrived. Finally, though, they were eliminated east of the Mississippi, and now survive in huntable numbers only in the true, mostly treeless grasslands of Oklahoma, Kansas, Nebraska, and South Dakota.

There they had burgeoned in uncountable numbers for a time—indeed, the time Sandys writes about, from the 1880s through the 1920s—on the seeds of broomsedge and bluestem, wild berries, and the mast produced by bur and blackjack oaks, along with what small agricultural grains they could snatch from the ever-expanding farmland. Often in the winter they would congregate wherever oaks could be found in "great musterings" of a thousand, perhaps two thousand birds each. But a combination of bad winters, dust storms, and possibly the overhunting triggered by the Depression of the 1930s sent prairie grouse populations everywhere spinning downward toward doom.

Today, a map of remaining prairie chicken distribution resembles a scattering of puny, amoebalike blotches within the outline of their former range. The greatest number are found in the Flint Hills and adjacent grasslands of east-central Kansas, where in 1967 they were estimated at 750,000 strong. In that same year, Nebraska and South Dakota could count perhaps 100,000 birds apiece. Remnant, and usually protected, breeding populations remain in North Dakota, Minnesota, Wisconsin, Michigan, Illinois, and Missouri. Oklahoma, to its credit, has been restocking greater prairie chickens in its northeastern grasslands, and there the population is growing. But in Minnesota, where 411,900 of the birds were killed during the peak-population year of 1925, only 5,000 remained a mere forty years later.

By 1982, no more than 700 prairie chickens survived in Wisconsin, Michigan, and Illinois—"as out of place as wampum on Wall Street," wrote the late John Madson in his poignant study of the tallgrass prairie, *Where the Sky Began* (Sierra Club Books, 1985). "They are relicts that have long outlived the original prairies that brought them into existence. They now exist on artificial prairies that are their final strongholds east of the Mississippi—little reliquaries of flocks that once spanned the prairie horizons."

Back during the golden age of chicken shooting, Edwyn Sandys once killed, over a three-day period, one hundred straight birds with as many shots from his trusty, double ejector-gun on the rolling plains of South Dakota—sure testimony to the ease of shooting big, close-holding, raggedly-flushing birds in open country. But he found greater joy in hunting them on the small, hilly, brush-rimmed prairie "islands" of southern Wisconsin where I grew up forty years later and was first turned on to bird hunting by that same "drum-eared lover," *Tympanuchus cupido.*

"Much of the timber of these hillsides is small oak, and the general appearance is parklike," he wrote. "On such ground the shooting is excellent, there being just enough trees to keep a man keen and careful.

Many other places present a snarl of low scrub-oak and hazels, seldom more than waist-high. In such cover the chickens lie like quail, and a good shot can walk them up singly and drop bird after bird till his coat can hold no more—then hey! for the following wagon, to deposit therein the slain, and to resume the beat till the coat is again too heavy for comfort. . . . It is quite true that the number of birds and the possible bags could never rival the possiblities of the mighty grass-lands farther west, yet a gun could stop from a dozen to three times that number of birds during a day of hard work, and could a sports-man desire more? Your true sportsman is an artist, not a butcher. . . ."

Well, if you say so, Eddie. As a kid, hunting with my single-shot 28-gauge Savage behind a pair of half-wild Irish setters, I counted myself lucky to kill three or four birds a day, out of perhaps three covey rises of twenty or thirty birds each. Only a few times did I manage a double from the same flock. When dogs pin a covey of chickens, the birds rarely flush simultaneously. Unlike quail, they get up in small, straggling groups, by fours and twos and singles, allowing a cool shot carrying a double gun with crisp ejectors to drop a pair, break the gun, stuff in a couple more shells, and if he's lucky kill yet another brace as the final birds jump tardily skyward. If you're using a single-shot gun with no ejector, it's more than twice as hard to score a double.

I can still recall as if it were yesterday the last double I killed on the greater prairie chickens of southern Wisconsin. I was fifteen years old at the time. It was one of "those occasional warm, windless, sleepy spells" of which Sandys had written so fondly at the turn of the cen-tury, "so strongly suggestive of the genuine Indian summer of the East. Then the fully matured birds lie like dead things, but rise swift and strong and go whizzing away on what surely will prove very long flights unless the lead prevents."

On that balmy October morning I was clad in my stylish warm-weather hunting garb—high-top Keds caked with mud, faded Levi's, a ripped white T-shirt that bore no logo in those days before we all became walking billboards, and a ragged straw fedora my dad had passed along to me. In lieu of a gamebag, I carried an empty flour sack looped to my belt. Rusty, the male Irish setter who usually accompanied me, was off on personal business that Saturday—perhaps a bitch in heat somewhere in the neighborhood—but wise old Belle, his partner in crime, trotted ahead as I pounded the thousand acres of virgin tallgrass prairie that still remained between my house and the river bottom.

I suspected, and Belle soon confirmed, that the flock of chickens we'd jumped a week earlier was still "using" in the bluestem near a brush-choked gully that led down to the river. The birds rarely fed more than a few hundred yards from the gully's edge, so that they could quickly fly back into the tangled sumac, scrub oak, and crabapple jungle when threatened. Our strategy, as usual, was to circle wide to the east and pussyfoot our way along the edge of the brush until we were between the birds and their hidey-hole, at which point I'd send Belle into the tall grass to seek a point. What little breeze there was that day blew from the northwest, and soon Belle's red, feathered tail told me she had whiffed our prey. After loading the gun and taking a spare shell from my pants pocket to hold between the fingers of my fore-end hand for a fast reload, I hied the old girl on.

A hundred yards in, she locked up—head low, ears cocked, tail high, and trembling. I came up behind her, my nerves as always atingle, as if I were walking into a minefield laced with Bouncing Betties. As I passed her, she broke point and raced in ahead of me, flushing the flock. Five birds jumped up, and I dropped the trailer in a flurry of white and brown feathers, then three more flushed as I broke the gun open, groped with clumsy fingers to free the empty casing, and fumbled the second shell into the gun. The second group of three was well out of range by the time I snapped the gun shut, but then a single erupted from the grass and flailed away into the breeze. I centered it, angling away to my right, and it tumbled to earth with a satisfying thump. Finally, as I stood there, too stunned even to grin at my good luck so far, much less to reload the Savage, Belle flushed the remaining six birds in the covey. I watched them out of sight, alternately beating and gliding on a long, swift slant for the wood-edged river bottom half a mile away.

Belle brought me the first bird, and as I dropped it in the flour sack an angry voice ruptured my joy.

"Hey, kid! Whatcha doin'? Ya damn near shot us!"

Two red-faced men in work clothes came stomping toward me through the bluestem. They carried surveying gear—theodolite, chain, rod, clipboards.

"Bird hunting," I said. And quickly reloaded the Savage, remembering my run-in with tramps while duck hunting near the railroad tracks the previous fall. "I didn't know there was anyone else in the field. And I was shooting high, anyway—you weren't in any danger."

"Don't gimme none of your lip," the man yelled. "We work for the county, I oughtta report you. There's a road going in here, and a bunch of new houses, starting next spring. Now get your ass outta here before I call a cop. No hunting allowed!" He was visibly shaking, whether with rage or fear I couldn't tell. His partner looked at the ground, clearly embarrassed.

Belle brought me the second bird. I put it in the sack and turned to go.

"Maybe you oughta give me those birds," the man hollered after me as I walked back toward the distant road. I just kept going. "Hey, kid! What's your name—I'm gonna report you!"

I turned again and looked at him, the gun upright in one hand but angled slightly in his direction. I gave him the finger and marched on.

But it was a sour way to end a love affair with a splendid game bird, and for years afterward—while I hunted other birds in other places—the memory of that seemingly final encounter with prairie chickens still rankled. So last year, when the opportunity arose to spend a day on the South Dakota grasslands in pursuit of prairie grouse, I had to do it. I'd been hunting pheasants at the Paul A. Nelson Farm near Gettysburg, South Dakota—part of a "focus group" of readers and writers arranged by *Shooting Sportsman Magazine*, for which I write a bimonthly column called "The Dawn Patrol."

The shooting at Nelson's was splendid—as good as or better than it had been at Hendry Gobel's place during my last pheasant hunt in South Dakota, nearly half a century earlier—and the readers proved a totally delightful, and totally focused, assortment of men and women from all over the country, all united in their love of good guns and magnificent game birds. Two groups of twenty readers apiece were shooting with us, and during the transition day between them, we writers had a day off. What better way to spend it than bird hunting? Ralph Stuart, editor of *SSM*; Michael McIntosh, America's premier writer on the subject of fine double shotguns; and I arranged to spend the day afield with a local guide named Bob Tinker and his English setters.

At the crack of dawn on that memorable Wednesday, we rendezvoused with Tinker at his home on the outskirts of Pierre. "Don't tell anyone where we're hunting," Tinker said as we drove out of town. He's a tall, rangy, dark-bearded man of thirty-five, a former track star (hurdles) with the legs to prove it, affable and witty but understandably anxious to protect the exclusivity of his hunting grounds. "We'll see mixed coveys of sharptails and prairie chickens; the limit is three birds per gun of either species."

I flashed on Edwyn Sandys, and his admonition to the "artist" sportsman to limit his kill to three *dozen* chickens a day.

"Where I'm taking you," Tinker continued, "the birds haven't been pressured much yet this season. They ought to hold tight in front of a point, no wild flushes. The sharpies, if you haven't hunted them before, they're a bit slimmer and lighter than the chickens, with short, pointed tails—kinda like immature hen pheasants. You can tell the chickens by their strong barring, dark brown and almost white on their breasts and wings. . . . Hey, look, there go some sharptails!"

The birds, maybe eight or ten of them, had flushed from a roadside ditch as Bob's truck roared past. They flew with the same flap-flap . . . glide wingbeat of chickens, and put down in the short grass a few hundred yards from the gravel road. "Let's have a crack at them," Tinker said.

While we broke out our guns and loaded up, Bob released his senior setter from the dog box—a handsome, square-headed chap named Colt. We circled downwind and well into the prairie, then hunted back toward where the birds had landed, Colt quartering well before us, head up, sampling the wind. But we'd walked too far in from the road, and suddenly the birds flushed wild, out of range to our left. They whizzed a long, long way, as they will "unless the lead prevents."

Just as well, I felt—the encounter had seemed too much like road hunting for my effete eastern taste, spotting the birds from the truck, dismounting, and walking them up where they'd landed. Then I remembered Saint Sandys' wagons, his one-armed and no-legged hunters, and had to laugh at my sanctimony. For all Tinker knew, our legs were made of Silly Putty.

"Okay," Bob said as we trudged back to the truck, "at least we got the kinks out."

By now the sun was well clear of the flat horizon and the prairie faded from a rosy gold glow to the flat yellowish white of autumn-dried grass, blotched in spots—like the map of fin-de-siècle prairie chicken distribution—with squiggles of green and purple where water still encouraged some life. Well away from the highway to Pierre, well into the wild prairie, we stopped on a lonely, poorly maintained dirt road overlooking a rolling sea of grass, stretching vast and seemingly lifeless to the west until a dusty horizon met the wind-streaked sky. A lone hawk circled far in the distance.

I took a deep breath, recalling the Wisconsin of my boyhood. And with the first step away from the road, I was back there. . . . What it's about: Walking the grasslands near dawn. Oh sure, the day would become a scorcher, with the mercury touching 90, but in that hour following sunrise the air was still crisp and fresh. The prairie rolled out before us, an endless scroll, and the dogs—this time Bob's younger setters, named Rajah, Scorch, and Aussie—were still frisky, all of us delighted to be alive and hunting up a morning like this.

And when Scorch locked on point a short while later, down near a damp green line of streambed, well beyond sight of the truck or the road, with only the hawk still circling overhead, nearer now, and the other dogs honored his frozen point, and Bob walked in, and the birds started getting up—big chunky birds, barred brown and white, with that initial leap well into the sky, that flurry of primaries—I had been there long, long before. I shot once, twice. The wind muffled the sound. Two birds fell. And I stood there again as I had long ago, awed and delighted, and too stunned at my good luck to reload.

More birds got up, of course, but I didn't shoot at them.

"You could have had three from that bunch, if you'd only reloaded," Bob Tinker said when the smoke cleared. "*Your limit,* man."

"I guess," I said, and let it go at that.

But it was the first double I'd shot on prairie chickens in nearly half a century. I guess I didn't want to spoil the symmetry.

We pounded a long way that day, over windy, wondrous prairies. We flushed three more big coveys of prairie grouse, and a few singles and doubles. We filled our tags. Ralph Stuart, heeding Tinker's advice, managed to take his whole limit from a single covey flush, killing two birds on the initial rise, then reloading his over-and-under like some sort of sleight-of-hand artist and nailing a third as the last of the stragglers got up. Michael McIntosh, demonstrating that he can shoot with the same wizardry that marks his writing, managed somehow to kill two chickens with a single shot on the final covey rise of the day. "An appropriately named Scotch double," the silver-bearded Caledonian allowed.

That night I slept well. The memory of the red-faced surveyor who'd spoiled my last hunt for prairie hens had been laid to rest, his image erased by this final South Dakota double.

Yes, the surveyor had done his work, all right. The following spring the virgin prairie across from my home in Wisconsin quickly turned into a housing subdivision. Where I'd once been awakened by the distant boom of courtship rites as practiced by the Drum-Eared Lover, now all I heard was the whirr of lawn mowers and the thump of backyard basketballs, pleasant enough in their own suburban way, but not quite the same.

"It is a lonely, wild sound made by a lonely wild bird," wrote my friend John Madson of *Tympanuchus cupido*'s mating rituals. "It has the quality of an ancient wind blowing across the smokeflap of a wickiup—companion noise to an Indian courting flute and the drum of unshod pony hooves on bluestem sod. In all of modern America, there is no more lost, plaintive, old-time sound than the booming of a native prairie chicken. And when it is gone, it shall be gone forever. All our television will not bring it back, and none of our spacecraft can take us to where it vanished. It is the last fading voice of the prairie wilderness, echoing after the lost clouds of curlews and plovers, crying farewell."

In the Drowned Lands

"THIS IS IT?" Cargill asked. He hefted the antique firearm in his soft city hands and looked incredulously at the lawyer. "You hauled me all the way up here to the sticks—a whole day away from New York—just to tell me that I've inherited a . . . *a fowling-piece?*"

"You are his only heir," the attorney said patiently for the tenth or twelfth time. "Your uncle was an eccentric man, set in his ways. As I explained in my letter, his will required your presence, in person, at the reading if you were to inherit. Otherwise his estate would go to various charities. Besides, it's not just the shotgun, Mr. Cargill. There's also the land, the house, and all of its contents."

"Yeah, right," Cargill said. "For what it's worth. Tell me, Counsellor, what *is* it worth?"

"Well," the lawyer said, clearing his throat, "to tell you the truth, Mr. Cargill, not a whole lot at present. We're too far from the interstate and the mountains for this property to interest any big-time developers. Mingo Mills, the nearest town of any size, is losing population. So's the whole region, as you must have noticed during our drive up here. There's no industry to speak of and even the farms are failing. I doubt you could find a ready buyer for the place in this current economy in less than a year's time, but if you were to hold onto the place for a while, who knows? At least the taxes aren't ruinous."

Cargill looked down at the shotgun. A bespoke pre–Civil War caplock, the lawyer had said, 14 gauge, made by W. W. Greener of London. Actually it was rather a handsome piece, Cargill thought. Long, slim barrels the glossy black of rich coffee, sinuous gooseneck hammers of case-hardened iron as bright as buffed nickel, the rose-and-scroll engraving on the side plates elegant and finely cut, a diamond of ancient ivory embedded at the tip of its rosewood forearm, and two others of somewhat larger size on either side of the oil-finished, tiger maple stock. It had been years—decades—since he'd last held a shotgun, much less fired one. On a sudden whim he threw the gun to his shoulder. It came up light and smoothly balanced, a perfect fit, the ivory bead at the end of the tapering 30-inch barrels locked firmly on the amber eye of a woodcock mounted in frozen flight at one dim corner of the study. . . .

Francis Edmond Cargill, an accountant, lived and worked in Manhattan. A widower now for some twenty years, ailing, dead at heart, and childless to boot, he had little left to him but his profession, and that was dwindling away year by year as his clients passed on. Soon he would join them, of that he was sure. *Ho hum.* One day recently he'd received a letter from an upstate attorney advising him that he'd been named sole beneficiary in the will of a bachelor uncle whom he hadn't seen or talked to in nearly half a century. Indeed he'd supposed that Colonel Elijah Cargill was long since dead, if he'd thought of him at all. The lawyer, whose name was J. G. Braithwaite, asked Francis Cargill to come upstate for the reading of the will. "The inheritance is substantial," he'd written. "I'm afraid I can't tell you just now what the legacy comprises. I suppose your uncle wished it to be a surprise. A codicil to his will, written shortly before his death, specifies that you must be present in the old man's house when it's read."

It was early autumn but still hot and humid in midtown, and Cargill was only too grateful for a chance to get out of the city for a day or two. That Friday morning he packed an overnight bag and caught the 10:15 train from Grand Central to Beacon where Braithwaite, a dry, soft-spoken, rather elderly fellow, picked him up in an equally ancient Plymouth station wagon. They'd crossed the Hudson River, then headed southwest on country roads into the foothills of the Catskill range.

It was a pretty drive through rolling, sparsely settled farm country with only a few small villages marking the way. They drove past marshes, alder brakes, abandoned barns and farmhouses, old orchards, stands of aspen and pine and mixed hardwoods, then down a lonely two-lane black-top road that eventually petered out into gravel.

"We're on the edge of what used to be called the Drowned Lands," Braithwaite said. "It was a huge, level tract of wild country, kind of a floodplain of the Walkill River—all brakes and thickets interspersed with bog meadow and grassland, with here and there a stand of open timber. Most of it's drained and cut over now, but your uncle kept his piece pretty much as it was in the old days. Are you a bird hunter, Mr. Cargill?"

"Used to be," Cargill said. "When I was a boy I sometimes shot with my uncle. But I drifted away from it when he moved up here and, later, I went to work in the city. Can't say that I miss it, though."

"Back in the nineteenth century this was splendid woodcock coun-try," Braithwaite continued. "In 1839, a Englishman named Henry William Herbert used to shoot here with a friend of his from the town of Warwick—a huge fellow named Mr. Ward, who weighed three hun-dred pounds and shot a single-barreled Westley Richards. Even with those handicaps they often killed close to a hundred woodcock a day between them. A year or so later, Herbert and another friend, probably shooting a double gun, bagged a hundred and twenty-five on one day and another seventy the following morning, not including forty or fifty birds their retrievers couldn't find."

"Game hogs," Cargill said. He winced and stretched his legs. Arthritis takes it toll. "Sheer waste. What could they do with that many birds?"

"Sold them on the New York market, no doubt. It was legal back then."

"More's the pity," Cargill said. "No wonder there's nothing left."

Braithwaite merely grunted.

It was late afternoon when they turned off the main road into a rutted driveway winding through deep woods. A startled deer leaped ahead of them down the track, then broke into the forest, its white tail flagging. Farther on they flushed a small covey of ruffed grouse that had been dusting at the side of the road. They passed ponds etched with the rings of rising fish, on one of which Francis thought he saw a family of wood ducks, before coming to a stop before a small, slate-roofed fieldstone cottage.

"Your uncle always referred to the house as his 'shooting box,'" the lawyer said. "An English country gentleman's term, I guess." Two great, feathery white pines, their upper branches sighing in a cooling breeze, flanked the north side at either end. "Grandmother and Grandfather trees, your uncle called them," Braithwaite explained, "planted ages ago to break the wind from the storms that sweep down now and again from the Catskills."

From somewhere behind the house came the anxious barking of dogs. "The kennel's back there," Braithwaite said. "I've been feeding and watering the dogs every day since your uncle's death." He cleared his throat. "Only two of them," he added quickly. "I hadn't really the heart to put them down."

The lawyer unlocked the door and ushered Cargill inside. "The Colonel didn't hold much with electricity," Braithwaite apologized, lighting a coach lamp mounted in a pewter sconce on one wall of the entry hall. "I misdoubt there's three lightbulbs in the whole place." English sporting prints lined the hallway, along with the large, spread fans of numerous ruffed grouse. "Your uncle was certainly a keen wing-shot," Braithwaite said. "Even at the end, well into his nineties, the folks hereabouts would see him afield in all kinds of weather with his dogs and his gun."

Braithwaite led the way over lustrous, random-width pine floorboards through a cavernous living room sparsely scattered with throw rugs and a few pieces of overstuffed furniture upholstered in dark, well-oiled leather. The mounted heads of two big-antlered deer and a single black bear gazed down solemnly from the walls, their glass eyes glinting in the dusky green light from a leaded window. Again Braithwaite stopped, this time to light a pair of ornate kerosene lamps that stood on curly maple end tables beside an easy chair. A huge fieldstone fireplace dominated one end of the room. From it blew a whiff of cold ashes.

"In here, please," Braithwaite said, ushering Cargill into a book-lined study. "Your uncle called this his Game Room. If you could wait here a moment, I have to call my office." Cargill studied the bookshelves. Mostly sporting volumes from the nineteenth century by authors he'd never heard of. *British Rural Sports* by someone who called himself "Stonehenge," *Dinks on the Dog*, Maupassant's *Contes de la bécasse*, Frank Forester's *The Field Sports of America* in two volumes, and another by the same author entitled *The Warwick Woodlands*. *Ho hum*, he thought. The rear window of the Game Room looked westward into the backyard—to a handsome fieldstone barn with a cupola; a long, wire-enclosed shed, which he took to be the kennel; some other smaller outbuildings; and behind them, visible through the beginnings of the woods, what appeared to be a large pond or lake. Beyond it, nothing but flat, endless woodland broken here and there by expanses of bog meadow and dense stands of alder. Not a house nor another barn could he see, clear to the horizon. He turned back as Braithwaite entered the room.

"Let's get on with it," the lawyer said, suddenly all business. "The reading of the will." He pulled a sheet of foolscap from his briefcase and began: "I, Elijah Worthington Cargill, late Colonel, U.S. Army, being of sound mind. . . ." It was as Braithwaite had suggested earlier— the land, the house, and all the possessions within it, et cetera. Including the dogs and the Greener. . . .

After Braithwaite left, promising to return on Monday morning to drive Cargill back to the station at Beacon, Francis poured himself a glass of sherry from a decanter he found in the Game Room and began to scout his new pied-à-terre. His stiff legs needed stretching. The house certainly appeared to be in sound shape—no leaks, no water stains on the beamed ceilings, no sagging floorboards or crumbling walls—though with nothing by the way of modern conveniences. The kitchen was dominated by a huge, oldfashioned icebox—cooled literally by ice, great sawdust-flecked, opaque blocks of it, installed beneath the shelves; but it was well stocked, no doubt by Braithwaite, with fresh eggs, butter, milk, a pound of coffee, assorted vegetables and fruit, as well as some steaks and chops for Cargill's weekend meals. The sink faucet had to be charged by a hand pump, but the water was cold and sweet. The cupboards contained some fine blue-and-white china and a pebbled stoneware coffeepot. The stove, Cargill saw, was wood-fired, but there were plenty of kindling and split-hardwood chunks in a bin that stood beside it. He figured he could manage.

A kitchen table of solid oak stood on curved, hand-carved legs beside the west-facing window. On it stood another of the seemingly ubiquitous kerosene lamps. Was there no electric light in this house? Cargill circulated through the rooms, pausing to contemplate the bedroom with its brass four-poster and a tall armoire still filled with his uncle's clothing. Nowhere could he find a light switch; nowhere a single bulb. Nor a telephone. How could Braithwaite have called his office? Perhaps he'd had a cellular phone in his briefcase. Cargill went back out to the front door and peered down the driveway. He could swear he'd seen utility poles and power lines on the drive in. He must have imagined them. There were none, no power at all coming into the house from any direction. Well, it was a long way from the highway; no doubt the Colonel, a great believer in personal economies, had chosen not to foot the bill for installing poles and cables. He was a parsimonious old coot, Cargill recalled.

His sherry glass was empty and he went back to the Game Room to replenish it. Beside the decanter stood a humidor he hadn't noticed before. From it he took a long, thick, green cigar, not at all dry when he lit it, and as fragrant as any Havana he'd smoked when his wife would still allow him that pleasure. Puffing away grandly, he swung through the kitchen, found an icepick—God, it had been a long time since he'd used one—and chipped off a few shards of ice to add to his drink. He sat at the kitchen table and thought back on what he could remember of his uncle.

Cargill had found him to be a mysterious and romantic figure the few times he'd met the man during his boyhood. Uncle Eli—tall, slim, with dark, flashing eyes and a ready if somewhat cynical laugh—was his father's younger brother, the black sheep of the sober, God-fearing, and industrious Cargill family. As a boy he'd run off to find his fortune in Mexico but had ended up in the Mexican cavalry instead, fighting Pancho Villa. When America entered the Great War, he'd enlisted as a common soldier; by Armistice Day he'd risen to the rank of captain. Between the wars he'd served in some hush-hush capacity as a military intelligence officer, traveling frequently to Africa, the Middle East, the South Seas, Asia, and Latin America. On his rare visits to the family home in Oyster Bay, he told fascinating tales of Chinese bandits and big-game hunts in the Sudan, of diving for pearl shell in the far Paumotus or crossing the Empty Quarter of Arabia on camelback, of frozen toes in the heights of the sunny Andes and (sotto voce, over cigars and brandy after the ladies had left the room) of the smooth-bellied charms of those legendary Moroccan "dancing girls" called *ouled naïls*.

During World War II he'd returned to the infantry, commanding first a battalion, then a regiment, in North Africa, Italy, and finally France. He'd been badly wounded in the Hürtgen Forest but never spoke of it. After the war, Cargill had seen him only once. He was a changed man. They'd shared a duck blind one sleet-slashed morning on Long Island Sound. A bleak, bang-up day, the sky close, cold and writhing as low as a snake's belly, ducks everywhere—bluebills they were, Cargill remembered, greater scaup, ripping suddenly out of the murk to cup unheeding into the decoy spread. From all around them came the banging of other guns, unseen in the fog. Cargill had shot well, with the hot blood of youth, the big Browning's jolt lighting a fire in his heart, dropping doubles on nearly every toll, once a triple, the ducks splashing dead, loose-feathered, wings all asprawl in the black racing chop, one, two, three, and his uncle's fierce Chessie—yes, Rommel was his name—launching like a torpedo from the blind to fetch them back. But the Colonel had shot only once, killing a high single that was barely visible through the cloud scud; the bird tumbled end for end, like the footage Cargill had seen of flak-torn kamikazes over Okinawa, and splashed down close to the blind. It lay on its back, its broad black feet flailing weakly at the sky. "He's waving good-bye to life," the Colonel said. Cargill had looked over at him, amazed at this sign of sentiment in the heretofore laughing warrior.

"Too much death, too many people," Uncle Eli continued. There were tears in his eyes. "I'm leaving the army, Frankie. Leaving the whole damned twentieth century. It's time to call retreat." Rommel had lain his huge head on the Colonel's leg and groaned in sympathy.

As if reading Cargill's memories, the dogs in the kennel renewed their own whining. He walked out behind the house. There were two of them, as the lawyer had said, bitch and dog, but of a breed that Cargill had never seen before. They looked like outsized springer spaniels, but solid white in color, heavier boned and bodied, shorter in the legs, with longer ears, rougher coats, and broader noses than any spaniel of Cargill's acquaintance. Their heads were huge, almost primitive looking, though their big, dark eyes were friendly, pleading for his company. He noticed that their water dishes were empty and, without thinking, unlatched the kennel door to refill them.

Immediately the spaniels bulled it open and lumbered off in the direction of the pond. Cargill hurried after them. But instead of drinking, the dogs aimed their big-bore muzzles earthward and began snuffling through the alder brakes that surrounded the water. Suddenly the bitch let loose a deep, plangent note. She froze in her tracks, looking back anxiously over her shoulder as Cargill rushed up. When he was twenty feet away, she pounced—and a woodcock whistled skyward in wild corkscrewing flight, followed an instant later by a second bird. Simultaneously the male spaniel made game, sounding off musically as his short tail buzzed with excitement; and as Cargill turned toward him, the big dog flushed yet another brace, no, a trio of woodcock. When no shots followed the flushes, both dogs gazed at him sadly, almost reproachfully, he thought. But they came in readily when he called them to heel. They both wore broad leather collars, on which Cargill noticed brass tags with the dogs' names elegantly engraved. The dog was called Sancho, the bitch Pansy.

"Good dogs," Cargill told them. "Tomorrow I promise I'll bring the gun." They grinned up at him, whining and nodding their heavy heads in eager approval. They knew the word "gun" sure enough.

Living in the city, Cargill had denied himself the pleasures of dog ownership for far too long, he realized. His wife, a fastidious if not indeed a fanatical housekeeper, had claimed to be allergic to them, and he'd never pressed the issue. Now he realized what he'd been missing. Rather then locking the spaniels back into their kennel, he brought them with him into the house, where over the next hour they proved themselves thoroughly housebroken. In the living room Pansy curled herself up on a throw rug at the foot of the easy chair while Sancho sprawled with a contented groan on the cool slates in front of the fireplace. Cargill poured himself another drink and pulled *Dinks on the Dog* from the library shelf. Seating himself comfortably in the leather chair, he flipped pages until he found what he sought. Pansy and Sancho were clumber spaniels, no doubt about it, the largest representatives of their sporting family, and also the slowest. Often called "the retired gentleman's shooting dog," the clumber was of French origin, having come to England in the mideighteenth century as a gift from the Duq de Noailles to the Duke of Newcastle, whose manorial estate in Nottinghamshire was called Clumber House. The breed's period of greatest popularity in Britain was between about 1850 and the beginning of World War I. The Victorian Golden Age. The clumber was the perfect dog for a retired military officer or civil servant on pension, well behaved in the house yet keen afield. A clumber could be taken to the small coverts and truck-garden plots on the outskirts of London. While the elderly retiree sat dreaming of past glories on his shooting stick, his dog would nose about slowly among the bracken and turnip tops, seeking foot scent and throwing tongue whenever it made game, then retrieving whatever its master managed to shoot. Sounds like the dog for me, Cargill thought, flexing his stiff knees. We'll see tomorrow.

"Hey, guys," he called to the dozing clumbers, "what say let's grill us a steak or two for supper?" He realized that he was slightly buzzed. Well, country air, unaccustomed cigar smoke, a few glasses of vino. . . .

It rained that night, a steady, gentle susurration that stirred him from the murk of sleep into the cool dark blue of its shallows. But when he awoke refreshed the following morning, Cargill couldn't find his clothes. He'd folded them neatly on the chair beside the armoire before retiring. Perhaps the dogs had dragged them away during the night. Soft-heartedly, perhaps foolishly, he'd allowed the clumbers to sleep on the floor at the foot of his bed. Well, he'd no doubt find the clothing some-where around the house. In any case he'd brought no leisurewear with him in his small bag. He opened the armoire to see what his uncle might provide in the way of a shooting kit. In a few minutes he was clad in a fine, long-collared chambray shirt, fustian knee breeks, leather leggings, rough cowhide ankle boots, a long paisley-patterned waistcoat, and a rus-set-hued shooting jacket of stout corduroy. On his head he clapped a low-crowned felt hat and studied himself in the full-length mirror mounted inside the armoire's door. Quite elegant, he decided. The perfect picture of a Victorian country gentleman about to embark on a day afield. The dogs agreed, yipping their approval as they danced clumsily at his feet. Oddly enough his own legs felt just fine today, no aches, no stiffness. Usually it took him half an hour to work out the kinks on arising. Now, still standing before the mirror, he executed a quick buck-and-wing in the mode of Fred Astaire, doffing his hat at the conclusion and bowing sardonically to his dim rust-colored image.

After breaking his fast with a slab of crusty country bread accom-panied by a thick slice of sharp, crumbly cheese—to hell with choles-terol nightmares—Cargill took his coffee to the Game Room where he examined the Greener more closely. On the desk he found a full pow-der flask and a shot pouch, both mounted with cut-off spouts that mea-sured the appropriate charges for loading the gun. Strange he hadn't noticed them yesterday. But then again everything had been so new, in its old-fashioned way. In the roomy pockets of his jacket he found a nipple wrench, a box of shot wads, and an oval capping device with a spring-loaded gate. He charged the Greener, tamping down three drams of fine-grained black powder with the brass-capped ramrod, then insert-ing a wad, a one-ounce charge of small birdshot, and another wad to hold it all in place, feeling somehow that he had done this before, though he couldn't recall ever having fired a muzzle-loader at any time in his misspent youth. He did not cap the platinum-lined vents that angled down into the barrels, however. He would wait for that until he was outside. At sight of the gun, and especially when Cargill began charging it, the spaniels had flopped down on the floor of the Game Room, whining in barely suppressed excitement.

"All right, my friends, let's get going," Cargill said. He slung the empty gamebag over his shoulder without thinking where it came from. The dogs lurched to their feet and led the way out of the house. A crisp morning, heavy frost on the green grass that still lay in shadow, a crust of ice on the black mire beside the pond. The swamp maples blazed crimson, the aspens gold, all muted by the purple of the alders. Mist rose from the pond and from the springs that laced the woodland. Music chimed somewhere, and he noticed that the small pewter bells on the collars of the dogs tinkled a marching rhythm.

Odd indeed, Cargill suddenly realized. He could swear those bells hadn't been there the day before. Nor during the night. He'd certainly have heard them when the dogs rolled over in their sleep. . . .

But he had no time to ponder the problem. They were making game, down in the alders again. Ticking the hammers to half-cock, Cargill snapped a pair of copper priming caps over the Greener's vents and, with the gun at a high port arms, hurried after the dogs. At his approach Sancho flushed a brace of woodcock. Cargill found the Greener floating to his shoulder, his thumb drew the hammers to full cock, the heavy barrels swung up through the rise, then the touch of the slender, taut triggers—through billows of white smoke he saw the birds fall. Instantly his hands found flask and pouch, as if of their own volition; the ramrod was out; and as the dogs lay flat on their bellies, he began reloading. Then three more woodcock, startled by the shots, flip-flapped belatedly up out of the alders and flashed away, deeper into the covert.

"Good Sancho," he heard himself saying. Then, with a casting motion of his free hand, "Fetch dead, boy!"

And the dog hied into the brake, returning quickly with two 'cock, one after the other—warm, soft, and russet-feathered, their long bills lolling, a bead of blood bright at the tip of one of them, their huge, dark eyes still wet and almost luminous. As he brought them in, two more woodcock flushed. Then another. Cargill laughed and watched them go. He raised the dead birds to his face, inhaling their hot, musky essence. The dogs gazed up at him in approval.

"Hunt on, my worthies," he said, and he was laughing as he hadn't in fifty years. "Hunt 'em up! Hunt 'em *all* up!"

Ahead of them lay the unspoiled mornings, crisp and cool and bright with the fire and steel of eternal autumn, punctuated only by brief white clouds of burnt powder, the slow cough of his smooth, steady barrels. Francis Cargill knew now that he would hunt all day, forever. The powder flask would never need refilling, the shot pouch would never go slack, nor would the birds ever cease to fly. It would rain only at night, of course. In his mind, as the mists blew clear, he could see the endless covert opening before him—the tight-laced woodcock brakes, the spongy snipe bogs, the sharp-thorned partridge lies, the grass-topped hills where he and his steadfast companions would pause to drink the cool breeze. Somewhere along the way, he was certain now, they would meet the Colonel. Together, dogs and men, they would push on into a world of blurred wings and broken rainbows.

Forever and ever, amen.